MW01251469

TOIL AND TREASURE IN ALASKA
The Memoirs of
Thomas J Thompson

Toil and Treasure in Alaska

The Memoirs of Thomas J Thompson

JOHN RITCHIE LTD
CHRISTIAN PUBLICATIONS

40 Beansburn, Kilmarnock, Scotland

ISBN-13: 978 1 904064 50 3
ISBN-10: 1 904064 50 7

Typeset by John Ritchie Ltd., Kilmarnock
Printed by Bell & Bain Ltd., Glasgow

Contents

Preface

The experiences recorded in this book which you are about to read are just a few of many in my 53 years of missionary work in Alaska.   God allotted that territory for us to labour in.

It would be impossible to even try to recall all the works of the Lord over all these years, but I trust what I have written here will exercise some young believers to launch out into the deep, and not just run along the beach, or just go from hall to hall.

As I write this, I have reached eighty-two years of age. I find my "tent", this physical body, showing the signs of wear. Like Samuel in 1 Samuel 7: 7-12, we have gone out from our Mizpah, and now we raise our Ebenezer and say, "Thus far, the Lord has helped us."

Looking forward, we say, "Maranatha!"

Thomas James "Tommy" Thompson
Anchorage, Alaska
2007

CHAPTER 1

The Start of the Journey

From my earliest upbringing in a Christian home, the sovereignty of God was at work preparing me for the future. In Galatians 1:15-16, the apostle Paul spoke about his ministry of the gospel and traced God's work all the way back to his mother's womb. This is a great encouragement to me as I review my own life.

I was born on January 31, 1925, in Belfast, Northern Ireland, the third of four children born to Thomas James "Jimmy" and Agnes Crooks Thompson. I was named after my father, but was called "Tommy" to avoid confusion. My brother Andrew and sister Eileen were older than me, and George came a couple years after me. Both my parents lived for Christ and raised their children in an atmosphere of reverence for God.

The Great Depression impacted my family when my father lost his job. Growing up in these hard conditions taught me lessons about God's provisions in answer to prayer. I often heard my parents pray to God to meet some particular need and He provided in ways that convinced me of His reality.

God revealed Himself even in my own life during a dark time of testing. As a young boy, I was stricken with meningitis. The doctor told my parents that he was sending me to Newtownards Hospital; only afterward he said it was "to save you from seeing him die".

"Lord, you know how much I love my wee Tommy," my mother prayed. "But if you want to take him, Thy will be done."

My father had to travel from Bangor to visit me. After eight days, in the mercy of God my fever went. A nurse inquired of my dad, "Are you baby Thompson's father?" Expecting the worst, he cautiously replied that he was. The nurse exclaimed, "Bring his clothes as soon as you can. He is better!" In my teens when I misbehaved, mother would say, "I never asked for you back." This always made me sorry for being her "black sheep" boy.

Even though we lived in the city, for some reason I became obsessed with wanting a donkey. Boldly and with childlike presumption, I asked my parents simply to buy me one. Of course, they couldn't, and told me so. Undeterred, I prayed to the Lord for a donkey. I wasn't surprised when, the next morning, a donkey stood in our backyard! It had escaped from its rightful owner and I could not keep it, but that experience still stands out today as a time when the Lord answered my childish prayer.

I loved to work. When I was 11 years old, I asked Mrs. Windrum if I could help her brush the pavement outside her grocery shop. She kindly consented, and soon that wee job progressed into helping her in the shop daily after school. When I left school at age 15, her husband gave me a job in his wholesale business.

While working for the Windrums, I also became indentured to marine work in the famous Harland &Wolff shipyard in Belfast. That was where the legendary *SS Titanic* was assembled many years before. I was assigned after five years to be a "marker off" on the *HMS Eagle*. I attended Belfast College of Technology, "The Tech", three nights a week. I never missed a day during my training.

In 1944, when I was 19 years old, I met Sadie Scott. She was born on December 12, 1927, in Belfast, the middle child of Sam and Margaret Scott. Bill was her older brother and Betty was her younger sister. Sadie was a lovely, bright, happy girl, and we fell in love. Sadie and I got married on March 30, 1946, when I was 21 and she was 17. Neither of us was saved at that time.

Shortly after we wed, the post-World War II economy and dearth of job opportunities in Northern Ireland caused us to make plans to emigrate to South Africa where the economy seemed more prosperous.

About this time, however, the Lord saved Sadie. This produced in me a profound awareness of my own sinful condition. I had been brought up by believing parents, but had never confessed Jesus Christ as my personal Saviour. In contrast, Sadie's parents were good people who raised their three children within the Church of Ireland, but they were not saved. Sadie was always virtuous and morally upright, but salvation made her more truly "a new creation" than ever before. For several months I was deeply convicted about my godly heritage in contrast to Sadie's, causing a deepening awareness of my sinnership before God.

One day at work, the conviction of my sins forced me to take a break. I got down on my knees in a toilet and asked God to save me. Two scriptures I had learned in my childhood gripped me: Genesis 6:3, "My Spirit shall not always strive with man," and Job 33:14, "For God speaketh once, yea twice, yet man perceiveth it not." There on my knees I realized that my prayer got no further than the ceiling. I had always known I was a sinner, but after rising up from my knees in that place, I felt with renewed conviction that I was really lost. These verses were fulfilled in my life and I turned away God's grace. I knew I was on my way to hell, and never again would God speak to me.

Disturbed beyond imagination, I made my way to the Scotts' home where we were living to save up money for emigrating.

By this time I was refusing to attend church meetings with Sadie. At dinner, she asked her father whether he would go to a church meeting with her that evening.

"Don't ask me," he replied, "Ask your husband."

"He won't go," said Sadie.

"Go on, ask me!" I said to my young wife.

I asked her to go up to the balcony, because in my agitated mind I thought I would be with Christians and nearer to heaven than I would ever be. Conviction by the Spirit of God had brought to me real hopelessness of self, ever since my prayer that day at work. During the meeting I never heard a word the preacher said, for I was in agony of despair. As I sat beside Sadie little did she realize what was going on beside her. The battle for my soul intensified. The Evil One whispered to me, "Don't get saved now; just wait. Besides, they will laugh at you in the shipyard."

But God spoke in grace. "This is your last chance. Choose now for heaven or hell." I then simply cast myself into the arms of Jesus my Lord without saying a word and I knew I was saved forevermore. The date was January 14, 1947. Sadie cried with me as I told her of my conversion.

We went over to tell my parents. I knocked on the door and Dad opened it. "What are you doing here so late, Son?" he asked.

With maternal prescience, my mother shouted from the kitchen, "He is saved, Daddy!"

"Are you Tommy?" Dad turned to me.

"Yes I am," I declared. "I have come for that Bible you said you had for me when I got saved."

Sadie and I were both baptized and then gathered in the name of the Lord Jesus with believers who met in Victoria Hall assembly in Belfast. What joyful relief had entered my soul, and after all these years it remains as fresh as ever. Each morning of my life I go back to that moment when God saved this lost sinner by His grace. I have never once doubted this great transaction which brought me salvation, for it was so real.

Mr and Mrs T Thompson, 1983

CHAPTER 2

South Africa and Beyond

Later in the year 1947, we sailed for Cape Town, South Africa, on board the *HMS Carnavon Castle*, which was still a troop ship. Now new ambitions filled our lives.

We went to the shipboard church service because that's what a Christian should do on Sunday. The Captain was the speaker. I had seen him before this and, alas, he was anything but a Christian. So now I was determined to bear a true witness for the Lord among the other passengers. We had met two Scottish Free Church ministers, and I asked one to try and get us a room to have our own gospel meetings. We were given the top deck and took Philippians for our study. The meeting was crowded every night and an "open for all" gathering made the trip happy. How wonderful to practise separation without isolation. It was on board the ship that the Lord showed what He saved me out of and from. Witnessing in love to Christ and away from any other influence, our hearts were now set on Christ. I vowed always to stay near a local assembly of likeminded believers who gather in the Lord's name alone.

Disembarking in Cape Town at the tip of the African continent, we made our way inland to the bustling, gold-mining metropolis of Johannesburg. There Alex and Eleanor Maxwell met us and kindly took us under their care. They fellowshipped with saints in a Boy Scout hall in the suburb of Rose Bank. We learned to serve the Lord there in Sunday School, Bible Readings and prayer meetings. After a meeting one Sunday, Mr Fellingham, a missionary, gave me a word of caution: "Young man, there are two things in Johannesburg: God or gold. If you go in for God, you will never worry about gold. If you go in for gold, you will be a casualty of no use to God."

At the first prayer meeting I was very frightened, for they prayed clockwise. Soon it would be my turn, and I had never prayed in public before. I even thought of excusing myself and leaving. Dear Mr George Smith rose and read from Romans 8:16,17 and said a few words which eased my nerves and gave me some courage to take part. From then on we longed to be more active in our work and witness for the Lord. However some in the meeting questioned the role of women in the church, church membership and reception, and other controversial items. I cast these questions on the Lord. Taking care not to have the attitude of "they do this in Ireland", I went to the Bible and had every question answered, revealing to me principles which I hold to this day.

It was during this time that the Lord blessed Sadie and me with our first two children. Brian was born in Johannesburg on September 16, 1948, and Billy on March 6, 1951.

I commenced Open Air meetings. These are meetings where several believers would gather on a sidewalk or other public open space and each in turn preach the gospel message to all who passed by. We saw people won for Christ in this way. I always wondered why some believers were reluctant to stand with us. One elder even sat in his car a distance away. Sometimes while preaching in the open air, shouts to shut up were hurled at us. One dear sister said, "Tommy we should not come here again, we are upsetting the people."

We also started meeting for Bible studies in people's homes, called "cottage meetings". One night, some residents of a home nearby attended and this contact opened the door for preaching the gospel each Thursday evening in the Rand Epileptic Home. We saw several of these men saved within about six weeks. When I left, this work was carried on by Oscar Hinds who came and helped at the beginning. Neither Hinds nor I would be regarded as good gospel preachers at the time, but someone once said, "Fools on fire are better than scholars on ice."

George Knowles, a missionary in Palestine, visited our assembly in Johannesburg. We were very impressed with his reports of the Lord's work in that region, as he exalted what Christ had done in Palestine and upper Egypt. At home that night we prayed, "Lord if you can do that with George Knowles, could you do something with us?" Thus began our exercise of heart as to where the Lord would have us go.

Shortly after this my firm transferred me to the beautiful city of Cape Town. There I served the Lord with heart and soul mostly with my dear coloured brethren. Series of Gospel meetings brought many souls to Christ. Syd Schlozh, a fervent full-time servant of God who worked in the country assemblies took me along with him and I loved the work. God blessed as souls were saved and saints built up. I thought this was where the Lord wanted us to serve.

I was invited to speak at a conference, but felt inadequate and refused. "Let us make that decision, Tommy," the conference organizers said. "Come and minister to the assembly and we will see." Their decision was that I should speak. I studied Exodus 31 to speak on "God's Servant" at the conference.

I had to meet Sadie at the train station and was late for the afternoon announcements, so I wasn't there to hear them announce that each speaker was limited to a half-hour. My turn came and standing behind the pulpit trembling, I started to preach and felt the Lord giving me help. As an inexperienced speaker, I had not at that time developed a sense of time passing, so unaware of the half hour time limit I went on and on and getting help. Joe Kerr was chairman of the conference and I heard him say something on the platform behind me. I thought he was saying, "Amen!" Softly, I felt a tug at my coat. It was Mr. Kerr. "Tommy, sit down," he whispered. "Your time is up." After that conference, I was invited to four assemblies to finish my message!

We lived in a lovely town called Fish Hoek, south of the city of Cape Town. We had a flat overlooking the beach and we were happy thinking the Lord wanted us to labour here in the Cape Province. I kept busy in the ministry of the gospel even as I worked hard for the Mobil Oil Company, conducting lunch hour meetings in factories and holding cottage meetings in homes in the evenings, seeing precious souls saved.

I commuted each morning to Cape Town on the train with Frank Hamilton. He gave me Assembly magazines to read which he had received from his brother Sam, a full-time servant of God in America. There I read an article by an elderly servant appealing for help in "the neglected northwest Alaska". I was quite transfixed. An impression came over me that the Lord was saying, "This is where I want you to go." But I became very uncertain and I began to question the reality of this experience, for I knew nothing about that part of the world. I went to enquire at the United States consulate in Cape Town, but the man there knew no more than me. He showed me books about Alaska, which was at the time still just a territory of the United States. The only thing I did learn was that there was fish, furs and freezing cold! The lack of information made me apprehensive.

Together Sadie and I prayed. I decided to ask those whom I knew to be honest and good assembly elders to share this exercise: Hugh Vine (brother of W.E. Vine), Joe Kerr, George Dennis, Alf Smith, David Morris and a few others. I asked the

Lord to show me that if this was not of Himself he would in some way hinder me from making a mistake. I went on serving the Lord as before, and more blessing came from Him as many souls were saved.

Some began to question our exercise of seeking God's will about our going to Alaska, and this became very discouraging. I wrote to William Rae about these problems. He was the aged servant whose article started this exercise, now living and ministering in the state of Washington. His reply was, "If it is of God then the devil will use any means to stop you."

Eventually the day came for several assemblies to gather to consider my commendation to the Lord for His work in Alaska. Without a word of dissent, six assemblies joined in commending us to the Lord.

I resigned from Mobil Oil. From that first step of faith, God made it clear that He would provide for us. Men who worked with me threw a farewell party and gave a gift of £100 to buy something to remind me of them. With this gift and my severance pay in my pocket, I left the office for the last time.

I sat down at the railway station and wondered how I would make it financially. I remember thinking, "this your last salary, there will be no more and what will I do?" Arriving home, Mr. and Mrs. Alexander were there having come to encourage us in our going forth. They had brought a dressed chicken, six corn on the cob, four tomatoes, and a 10-shilling note. No one will ever erase the memory of the grace of these dear coloured saints who strengthened me against my fears of the future. Many have been the tests since then, but as Alfred Cuff, former missionary for over 50 years in China, said, "Tommy, faith will always be tested , but will never be disappointed." He also gave me Nahum 1:7 "....He knoweth them who trust in Him", not them who *say* they trust in Him. These words have often comforted us in times of testing.

Selling our few earthly possessions was easy. Booking passage on the ship to England in the cheapest berths used up all my severance pay and the gift from my fellow workmen. I had barely enough money to pay for wee Billy's fare However while parting from my dear parents they gave us a gift that helped us reach Ireland by train and cross-channel boat. The Lord provided all the funds we needed. Sadie, Brian and Billy had another journey before them, to depart by ship first for Cobh in Ireland, then over the Atlantic to America, and ultimately Alaska.

One brother who took our few suitcases in his car to the ship in Capetown for the voyage to England was surely kin to Job's comforters. "Tommy, the Lord can use your mistake, for this is not of God!" he said. On board the ship, many dear Christians had come to see us off, while others still warned me, "The brethren in Ulster and America will not be interested in hearing you blow your horn about your call!"

CHAPTER 3

From Ulster to Alaska

Since we were all citizens of Great Britain and both Sadie and I were born in Northern Ireland, visas to America were easier for us to get in Belfast.

Our arrival in our homeland brought much joy to family and many friends. We began to meet with the Maranatha Assembly, and when we arrived I asked the elders not to read the part of the letter of commendation about going to Alaska, because of the caution I had received before I left Cape Town. When we had left Ireland in 1947 we were in fellowship with saints in Victoria Hall, which was very 'missionary minded', so I did not wish to fellowship there in case they would embrace us just because of our going to Alaska.

In the four months it took to obtain a visa for entry to Alaska, we worked happily with Maranatha Assembly, visiting hospitals and seeing souls saved. Soon I was invited for gospel meetings in other assemblies. Each week there was a five-pound note on the notice board in the Maranatha Hall which kept us supplied with food and transport. George Holmes of Ballyhackamore Assembly, which I had attended as a boy, asked me one day for morning tea. He kindly got us into the missionary home, with coals for heating it, during our stay in Ulster. He took me to a Christian coal merchant about the coal, and I said, "I don't like to do this, Mr Holmes!" He replied, "Tommy, one of the reasons the Lord has for us to remember Him weekly is because we could easily forget. I'm just reminding this brother of a need for the Lord!"

I was called to the American consulate for our visa interview. My brother Andy had emigrated to Chicago and stood as security for us. We answered the many questions to the satisfaction of the immigration officer. Then he asked about our financial support. Without pausing, I simply answered, "The usual church channels." He pondered this for a moment, and then said, "That's fine."

Questions regarding my church affiliation were tricky. I pointed outside the immigration office across the street to Victoria Memorial Hall and told the officer that was where I started my church fellowship. He smiled and said, "Here are your visas and the best of luck young man." I came away with worshipful praise and thanksgiving unto the Lord.

The saints at Maranatha Assembly joined in our commendation and gave us a lovely farewell a few nights before departure. Many spoke kind and encouraging words. They also gave us a nice monetary gift. However, I still did not have enough money for our fare. It seemed as if the devil was conspiring to keep us there indefinitely.

When we got back to the missionary home, there was an envelope on the table. Inside was enough money for our fare across the Atlantic. Full of thanksgiving we purchased all four tickets. Praise the Lord!

In those days, the ship to America set sail from Cobh, Ireland, more than 300 miles south of Belfast. Once again, the Lord provided a way for our family to get there. But as Isaiah once observed, God's ways are not our ways, and His thoughts are not our thoughts.

Abbey Booth was a dear brother in Christ, in fellowship in

21

Maranatha assembly, who also suffered from asthma that often kept him awake at night. One night he heard neighbors who were drinking and planning to go to Dublin by taxi for a binge of liquor. Abby thought, "If the devil can send them by taxi to Dublin, I'll send Tommy to Cobh by taxi."

I refused the offer of a taxi ride, but accepted train tickets to Cobh. When our happy young brothers in the Maranatha assembly heard we had everything we needed to get by train from Belfast to Cobh, they arranged to take us to the train station. The morning of departure arrived and Sadie and I were packed, ready to be picked up and taken to the train station. Imagine our surprise when brother Harry Mitchell pulled up outside our home, driving his horse-drawn coal cart! I know God must have a sense of humor because I must have made quite a spectacle, all loaded up with our few possessions being taken to the train station by horse. Sadie and the boys rode in Jim Graham's automobile. But, oh, how those dear saints encouraged us on our way!

On the train we met a lady who said she knew some of the people who sang their farewell to us. Hannah Holmes was going to America for a Christian congress. At Dublin the "jaunting car" driver saw our bags and decided he did not want to take Miss Holmes, us, and all our luggage at once.

"Two trips mister!" he called out.

"Well," I replied, "In London the English taxi driver took all the cases."

Not to be outdone by some English taxi driver, the proud Irishman nearly damaged his back hoisting all our cases up on his jaunting taxi, including Miss Holmes' ones. We were taken across the city to connect with another train. I had only American dollars with me now apart from the few English pounds Sadie had received from her parents for a night's stay in Cobh in a bed and breakfast place, and we had no idea of how much this would cost.

"I think I have more English pounds than is permitted," Miss Holmes remarked to me. "What should I do?" I exchanged her pounds for dollars - it was just enough to pay for the night's lodging in Cobh.

Arriving in New York City harbour on July 2, 1954, we did not know whether anyone would meet us. We knew no one. The ship's intercom barked out instructions for disembarkation and customs. "If you disembark with your luggage you cannot come on board again," was announced. It was late in the day. We decided to disembark and just commit ourselves into the Lord's hand. One of our cases was missing and custom's men were waiting on us. "Lord, please turn it up," was my prayer. I was constrained to go under the H sign and praise the Lord there it was.

Unknown to us, Tom Ball of Belfast had written ahead about us to Dave Zuidema of Midland Park Assembly in New Jersey. At 11.30 p.m., some people were allowed to come past the barrier to meet passengers. Dave came through. He saw the two white-haired boys described by Tom Ball in the letter, but standing next to them was Hannah Holmes. Sadie and I were looking for the lost luggage. Hannah had short hair, but Dave had been told Sadie had long hair. After looking about, Dave was perplexed as to "my wife's hair". He was about to depart without us. Then at the last minute, Sadie appeared with her lovely, long hair and came over to the boys. Dave quickly became a new friend and took us to his hospitable home in Midland Park.

We had only $6 in our family treasury and 6,000 miles to go. We looked to the Lord. I was asked to preach at a few meetings in the Midland Park Assembly and was happy to do so. Meanwhile, I booked a train called the "Pacemaker" to Chicago and was to pick up the tickets by Friday morning. On Thursday evening, the Midland Park Assembly gave me a gift that covered our fare to Chicago, with $20 surplus. We never even hinted to anyone about our need but only prayed to the Lord.

Dave and his wife, her name was also Sadie, took us to the train station and gave us a box of sandwiches, candy, soft drinks and other treats. I will never forget their love and encouragement.

My brother, Andy, met us in Chicago. At his home, a letter from William Rae awaited us with a cheque for $200 towards purchase of a car. A call also came from the 86th & Bishop Assembly inviting us to fellowship with them.

I walked up and down State Street in Chicago looking for a car. "That ain't even a deposit," one man said, when I told him I had $200 to spend.

Andy and his wife, Winkie, gladly drove us to the meetings and left us there. When I arrived at the 86th & Bishop Assembly that night, my only suit was wet with sweat. Dear George Eadie was our host for the night. After the meeting, he took us first to the home of John and Edith MacLelland where we had been invited to fellowship with them.

"Why do you look like a pull-through tonight?" Eadie asked me when he noticed my wrinkled and worn suit. "I spent all day looking for a car." "What kind of a car do you want?" they asked. "I'm not fussy." I replied.

"How much do you want to pay?" I replied, "Two hundred dollars." George Eadie, an Irishman, and John MacLelland, a Scotsman, erupted in howls of laughter. After composing himself, John MacLelland called his brother-in-law, Jim Bennett, who had a car dealership. MacLelland told him about my situation. The next morning, Jim Bennett arranged for me to purchase an old, wood-sided 1948 station wagon for $200. John MacLelland phoned me with this good news.

I was as pleased with that old car as much as if it were new. The previous owner had a flower delivery business and used to water the flowers in back of the station wagon. The moisture had caused holes, loose panels and gaps in the floorboards. I patched the holes, tightened the panels, threw on a coat of paint and did the best I could to make that old car "road worthy". I stood back and thanked the Lord for the car, and was assured it was ready for the road to Alaska.

I had a few meetings in the Chicago area, and a few dollars were squeezed into my hand. Sister Walker gave me four of my favorite potato bread for the road. Bill McCartney, also an Ulster man, gave me $100. Now we were on our way "north to the future". William Rae arranged an invitation from the Pattersons in Omaha, Nebraska, for us to stay overnight. They were our faithful helpers until they were called to higher service.

In Portland, Oregon, our benefactor William Rae met us and we had a lovely time with him and his deranged and crippled wife. After the meetings in the Stark Street Gospel Hall over the weekend, we headed north again.

Mr. and Mrs. Kazen welcomed us in Everett, Washington, yet another appointment made by William Rae. This dear couple took us to their home and treated us well. Sadie and the two boys had baths while I went to the meeting and preached. These saints in the assembly were so encouraged by the ministry that despite my protestations they passed the hat around for an offering. Feeling unworthy of their grace, I took the gift and put it in my pocket without looking at it, and thanked them from the bottom of my heart.

After a good breakfast, the Kazens loaded us with food for the day. We headed north again. At Mount Vernon, Washington, I purchased a box of margarine and a gallon of chemical toilet liquid. I had heard these were scarce in Alaska. As with many other things people told me about Alaska, afterward this proved untrue.

At Blaine, Washington, we had to pass through customs and immigration. "Anything to declare?" the officer asked. "Only a box of margarine" I replied. This caused him to take me to a more senior officer. "Why the box of margarine?" the senior officer wanted to know.

Apparently there was some margarine for butter smuggling going on. The customs officers sealed the box of margarine, gave us a paper that had to be signed when we exited Canada, and issued a stern warning about this "infraction". The first officer apologized for the long delay and waved us, and our sealed box of margarine, on with "the best of luck".

As I backed out of the parking spot, the customs officer came running over. "How much money do you have?" he asked.

My heart sank a little bit because I knew that to be allowed on the Alaska Highway you needed a good car and $300 per passenger. The car looked good and acceptable. I started to count my money. "Oh, go ahead," he said, pointing us through the gate before I had finished. "That's all right."

Later we tallied up the gift I had received from the assembly in Everett, plus what we already had. It amounted to $400. The Lord had once again taken us through.

> *"When all created streams are dry,*
> *His fullness is the same;*
> *May I with this be satisfied,*
> *And glory in His Name."*

William Rae's nephew, John, met us inside Canada and saw to

it that we were cared for. He introduced us to some believers in one of the Gospel Hall assemblies there. One dear brother in Christ looked at the tyres on our old wood-sided station wagon. "You will never make the highway with those tyres," he observed.

He kindly had four, brand-new, six-ply tyres mounted on the wheels. I kept the old tyres and tied them to the roof of the car. After about 400 miles on the Alaska Highway, all four new tyres blew out. I had the old original tyres put back on. They not only made it over the highway, but lasted for a few years in Alaska!

> "Foolish things, despised things,
> When weak in God's own hand,
> Can traverse over land and stones
> Where good tyres never can!"
>
> (T.J.T.)

The Alaska Highway was a rough, gravel road put through in haste by the U.S. Army after Japan began advancing up the Aleutian Chain of Alaska during World War II. We rode all day swirling in dust. To this day, Brian and Billy can remember when the floorboards gave out and they could see the road passing below the car. The price of petrol quickly drained our money. Stopping at night, we would pile out of the old car looking like something the cat dragged in, as the saying goes. But we forged ahead.

At Peace River, Yukon Territory, the river had washed away the road. The only way across was to drive up an embankment and rattle along over the railway bridge, high above the swift river. We crossed with fear. Sadie and Brian helped by just closing their eyes. Billy thought it was a great adventure; he kept our fear levels ratcheted up with a delighted narration of how high we were, and other scary details.

We made it over Peace River with nothing worse than elevated blood pressure. We kept our directions headed north and west. The Lord surely preserved us, especially at night when we pulled over to sleep along the side of the road. Large trucks would pass and make the car shake.

Just upon entering Alaska, the foot brake failed and I had to use the hand brake. I hand-braked to a stop at Scotty Creek. There a mechanic fixed a little copper pipe which had ruptured in the brake system. As we waited for the repairs, I gave out gospel tracts to many people there.

"I don't need one; I am a Christian," one man said as I offered him a tract. He was smoking a cigarette and drinking from a can of beer.

I drew close to him and said, "Sir you don't smell like one, or act like one!"

This led to an opportunity to talk to him about Christian sanctification as taught in Romans 6. Our conversation was respectful, and soon he felt comfortable enough to ask me personal questions about what kind of salary I was getting and my "Missionary Society".

When I answered that I was not getting any salary nor belonged to any society, he was very concerned about our future. He was amazed. "I never heard such a thing," he said. "God usually uses some church to support missionaries. I am a Christian, but nobody ever showed me this from the Bible. My pastor even smokes and has a beer, too." "That does not make it right for you," I replied.

I bid him farewell and went to pick up my car from the mechanic. I paid $9.50 for the work. As I was driving out of the repair shop's parking lot, the man I had been talking to came running towards us. I stopped and rolled down the window.

Tommy, will you do something for me?" he asked as he gasped for breath. "Yes, if I can," and he thrust a $10 bill in my hand. "Please keep it," he said.

There and then this act became a promise, and the Lord assured me, "I have brought you here and I will keep you here." Now I was fifty cents richer!

> *To keep me sure and steadfast,*
> *Within the narrow way,*
> *In love's obedience growing,*
> *More perfect day by day.*

I believe 1 Corinthians 9 gives scriptural principles concerning the liberty of a servant of God and his ministry, movements, maintenance, methods, and manifestation one day before God. I have sought to live in complete dependence upon the Lord. I have never even implied to be supported by anyone but the Lord. I take literally Matthew 6:33. "But seek ye first the kingdom of God, and His righteousness, and all these things shall be added to you."

Looking back, the Lord has been faithful in fulfilling His promise. He has never failed us once. Since leaving Mobil Oil, I have never earned wages and have never worked for a salary. I have lived a life of faith.

CHAPTER 4

Chitina, Alaska

The name "Alaska" derives from an Athabascan term for "the Great Land". This is no coincidence since Alaska is great in many ways.

Alaska measures 1,429 miles north to south, and more than 2,400 miles east to west. It has more than 6,640 miles of coastline, far more than the combined coastline of the continental United States. Beautiful mountains range across the land. Many peaks are snow-covered year around. Denali, sometimes known as Mt. McKinley, with an elevation of 20,320 feet, is the highest peak in North America.

Alaska is rich in natural resources. Minerals such as gold and copper have brought wealth and notoriety when unscrupulous prospectors came north to seek their fortunes. Of course, oil is now the biggest influence on the economy of Alaska.

When we arrived in 1954, Alaska was still a territory of the United States and governed by the federal government in Washington D.C. Alaska became the 49th state on January 3, 1959.

I have found the ways and life-rhythms of the Alaska native peoples to be most interesting. The native peoples in Alaska's interior are fishers and hunters. They hunt moose and caribou, but bear and rabbit are also eaten and their skins used for clothing or shelter. Blueberries, cranberries, salmonberries and raspberries are picked and stored for the winter months. Fish, especially salmon, are a major source of food and income.

Rivers are essential to the cycle of life because they provide the fish that are so central to sustaining life during the winter. In the summer, their icy-cold, fast-flowing, silt-filled waters can drown a person in seconds. Yet the native people have perfected techniques using nets and fish-wheels to safely harvest Red, Silver and King salmon. The salmon are cleaned and smoked, and then used throughout the long winters to feed families and teams of dogs. These massive rivers freeze to depths of four to five feet in the winter.

In the Athabascan Indian language, "chit" means "copper", and "na" means "river". Chitina (pronounced "chit-na") was the village to which God called us. Chitina is located on the banks of the mighty Copper River where it meets the smaller Chitina River in south-central Alaska, about 70 miles southeast of Glenallen, and about a 248-mile drive northward from the city of Anchorage.

Chitina is in an area populated by the Athabascan Indian people, the largest native people group in Alaska. Their history in Alaska goes back thousands of years. They live in many villages scattered hundreds of miles apart. Alaska was under Russia control and influence for 126 years. The United States Congress authorized the purchase of Alaska from Russia in 1867 for $7.2 million. Therefore the native culture was affected by these two international powers.

Like the Aleuts of the Aleutian Chain, the Tlingits of the Alaskan Panhandle, and the Eskimos of the western and northern coastal regions, the Athabascans were subjected to rough handling at the hands of the Russians and Americans. Russian and American adventurers brought foreign diseases and illnesses to Alaska. Many natives got sick and often died. It was not unusual for whole villages to be wiped out. Native girls and women were raped or bartered to unscrupulous traders to settle debts.

The Russian Orthodox Church imposed its beliefs on top of the Athabascan's native animist beliefs. Shaman, similar to witch doctors, played a key function in the village (including Chitina) by using mystical, demonic ceremonies to control the people. The result was a conflicting mixture of native mysticism and Russian Orthodox ritual that basically forced conformity through fear.

Hundreds of years later, the Russian influence can still be seen in some ways in remote areas. For instance, even now there are still village councils that are manipulated by local Russian Orthodox priests.

When the United States took over from Russia, its initial policy toward Alaska Natives was assimilation. This meant that the U.S. government discouraged the native languages and taught children exclusively in English. There was one central school drawing students from villages in that area. This meant that children had to leave home for their education, but then were not taught in their native tongue.

With American governmental control came American-style religious denominationalism which divided Alaska into areas of operation. Any native born in a denomination's pre-determined area of operation was considered by other groups to belong to that denomination. In the early 1900s, Chitina was a thriving boomtown. It catered to the construction of the Copper River & Northwestern Railway and was a centre for operations of the nearby Kennecott Mine. The mine closed in 1938 and the operations moved away. The railway was closed down.

By the time we arrived in the mid-1950s, Chitina was in decline. The natives were left without any means of support and this caused a hopeless spirit for them. Alcoholism became prevalent and some otherwise useful men became its victims. Today the estimated year-round population of Chitina is about 120, although tourism and fishing swell the population during summer months.

Our knowledge was very limited when the Lord first laid Alaska on our hearts. God had designs of grace toward the Chitina natives and was about to make His power known by the gospel.

View of Chitina, 1954

CHAPTER 5

Arriving in Chitina

We turned from the main highway onto a dirt road that led to Chitina, 40 miles away. It was a nightmare to drive. Tree logs had been embedded into the dirt road simply to make it passable.

Ascending a mountain on a winding, narrow road with many dangerous curves, we were nervous and wondered just how anyone could ever make it on this road. It was getting dark and we were still climbing the mountain road when suddenly we were in an area called Liberty Falls, a most beautiful spot.

Continuing our drive, we descended into a valley with swampy areas that took skillful driving to traverse. After passing several beautiful lakes, we were thankful to see the lights of Chitina. We breathed a sigh of relief. We were now at the place God allocated for us to work.

As we drove into this little village, we saw dilapidated buildings with eerie skeletons painted on the side. Stopping at a run-down store, we peered through the doorway and saw an unusual scene inside. With dim lighting, several weird, drunk men were standing around like ghouls.

Leaving the family inside the car, I went inside and asked for directions to the bunk house. A gentle type of man took me outside and kindly pointed it out to me. Looking around in the evening glow, the place looked like what the painted skeletons represented, "a ghost town"! Everything seemed run down; nothing looked new.

Driving toward the bunk house we saw that we would have to cross a creek by way of an old bridge. Suddenly we were mired in mud and slipping toward a swamp. Before I could get out of the car, two of the men from the store came and helped us get unstuck and over the bridge. I wondered what we had gotten ourselves into.

I knocked on the bunk house door. The door was opened by a kindly woman named Mrs. McKellar, known by everyone as Aunty May. She had come to Chitina from the Valley Christian Children's Home in Wasilla to work with the women of the village. She had heard of our coming and arranged for us to stay in the bunk house. She welcomed us in.

The place was lighted with an old oil lamp which cast a strange glow around our room. Regardless, we were all exhausted. Sadie and I were greatly relieved to tumble into a bed; Brian and Billy curled up in sleeping bags on an old couch. Unfazed, Sadie saw the funny side of it all and had a good chuckle at my apprehension.

When morning light came, we peeped out the window at our ghost town. Sadie helped Auntie May prepare a lovely breakfast. We had a good talk about plans for our accommodation. Another old building would have to make an apartment for Auntie May. I began soon to do this, and had her into a nice wee apartment.

I decided to survey Chitina and set out to walk around. I turned up an old road and came to the native village and soon began talking to them in their cabins. Joy filled my soul as I realized we were in the place to which the Lord called us. We felt bonded to these dear people and found out about many things that they learned to sustain their culture.

Living conditions called for lots of labor. Many other surprises awaited our learning. Since wood was essential for heating and cooking, I had to cut down trees, strip the branches, haul the logs home, cut them for length, and split them to useful size. It took four cords of wood to make it through the year. A cord is a pile measuring 4ft x 4ft x 8ft. This was a very burdensome task.

Water was brought in buckets from a spring at the side of a nearby creek. When winter cold froze the creek, Sadie or I had to break the ice with an axe. Our light came from a gas lamp and candles. Occasionally the old cynic O. J. Nelson ran his light plant for a few hours and this helped us with electric light. Toilet facilities were in an old outhouse over the side of the river!

We went to the store to buy bread. But by the time bread arrived from Anchorage or Fairbanks, it had started turning green. Sadie had never baked bread, but as a girl in Belfast she had won many awards for baking and sewing. She asked the Lord for guidance, and set about to make bread. She produced the best bread on earth. For years afterwards, even after we had moved to live in the city, the smell of fresh-baked bread was a regular part of our home. When Sadie went home to glory in 1984, she left me four loaves of her homemade bread!

These and many other difficulties in this primitive life surely added to Sadie's work, yet she never complained, "enduring hardness as a good soldier of Jesus Christ". Her record is on high and will bring the "well done".

A few years before we arrived, another missionary in the area had built a nice church building in Chitina. It was not being used and Auntie May opened it up for us. I started preaching services there. Behind the pulpit, I strung up a large canvas depicting Israel's journey from Egypt to Canaan and preached my first messages based on that wonderful narrative account. The conditions of the Israelites in Egypt resonated with the native people. Nearly all of them in the area came to the meetings. A few hardened alcoholics were among the very few who refused to come.

Alcoholism had many people in its grip. A sad example came when I was walking through the cutout road that led from the village to the Copper River. I walked past an abandoned boxcar. Hearing some sounds coming from inside it, I decided to investigate. Stepping up to the boxcar, I slid open the heavy door. I recoiled from the stench: a heavy mixture of alcohol and human waste. I could see the forms of three drunken men lying among empty beer cans and empty booze bottles. These were men who had reverted to hopelessness and gave up on life. I recognized one of the men as Joe Eskalida, a native whose father had been a local chief.

Seeing there was nothing I could do, I turned and kept walking. A short distance away I saw Tom Bell, another prominent native, and his son Pat, staggering along the road; they too were alcoholics. My heart ached for these men who had become enslaved by Satan's influence. I fell down and cried, "Lord, can you save these men?" God answered my cry by filling my heart with more resolve to use the Egypt-to-Canaan chart to preach the gospel every night of the week.

About three months after my encounters with the alcoholic men, a strange thing happened. One evening, a crowd of the natives of Chitina approached our bunkhouse. They simply came in, sat down and said nothing. (The way we had been raised in Ulster, if visitors come into your house you treat them like guests by chatting with them and perhaps offering them a cup of tea.) Sadie tried to be a gracious hostess according to what she knew, but her efforts at conversation were to no avail. We were perplexed, to say the least.

Sadie looked at me as if to say, "What do I do?" I did not know, either.

Suddenly, they all stood up and began placing many things on the table. Frozen fish, lots of frozen berries, bread, meat, a big cooking pot and several dessert goodies. Then just as quietly as they had arrived, they all turned and left. Sadie and I looked at each other, dumb-founded.

The next morning, I met one man and asked him about the generosity of the night before. His reply caused us tears of joy.

"We are glad you come live with us," he said in the broken English characteristic of the people there.

We could also say, "We sat where they sat."

CHAPTER 6

First Converts in Chitina

While we were preparing to leave Ulster, Mrs. Geddis, a missionary from Africa home on furlough, advised us to take along some schoolbooks to teach Brian. Since he had just reached school age, we took the advice. Little did we realize then but there was already a teacher living in Chitina and teaching the area children at the federally-funded Village Indian School. What a blessing when the teacher allowed Brian to enroll.

Even as God was working among the villagers, God was working in our family, too. The first convert was Brian. One day he asked Sadie how to be saved. Wisely, Sadie sat down with him and showed him passages of Scripture. That night he asked me how to be saved. I spoke about how salvation was like God's gift. I used a penny to illustrate about giving, receiving and accepting. He seemed to get help, and before falling asleep he was saved.

The next day Billy accompanied us as we walked Brian to school. On returning home he asked, "Daddy, can I have a saved penny?" A few years afterward he too was saved.

At that time the Lord saved several of the men I described as hardened alcoholics. Pat Bell tells his own story in his tract titled, "How God Saved Me" (see page 120).

Tom Bell, upon seeing his son Pat so changed, tried getting

saved his own way by going down a trail and spending some time alone in the woods. He came back and into his old life. One morning after leaving Brian at school, I felt led to visit Tom. Most villagers were in a never-ending cycle of debt to the storeowner O. A. Nelson. At one time or another Nelson owned or controlled nearly every piece of property and business in Chitina.

As I spoke to Tom, I used his debt to illustrate his state before God. Jesus paid the debt by His own blood on the cross.

"If I paid O. A. Nelson all your debt, what would you do?" I asked Tom.

"I would say thank you," Tom replied.

T Thompson with people from Chitina. Pat Bell extreme right, Tom Bell extreme left.

Tom suddenly dropped to his knees at his table and called upon God for salvation. From that moment he became a child of God; he never went back to his old lifestyle of alcohol and despair. Incredibly, Tom lived to be 90 years old and after his conversion took every opportunity to prove the power of God before all the natives. Before he was saved he and his son Pat would cut wood for a retired lady. When they had cut enough wood for a few dollars they went and bought wine and got drunk. After he was saved he went to her house and cut up all her wood. The woman went to pay him but he refused and said, "Me saved now." The lady asked me what I had done with him? I was able to tell her of God's power to save, but she cast it aside. Such was the power of God manifest that natives from villages from miles away started coming to hear the pure gospel message. Several of these were saved.

Another victory over Satan came in the life of Johnny Billum. Johnny's wife, Mollie, was in our fellowship and brought her children to all the meetings. Johnny was enslaved by alcohol and never darkened the door of our meetings. Often I would see him and his friends driving around the village in his old green car, all drunk as usual.

When I had witnessed to Johnny, he told me that he was a member of the Russian Orthodox Church and thought he was a Christian.

"Thompson, when I die I'm going to hold on like Jacob till the Lord blesses me," he explained.

"Johnny," I said, "The difference between Jacob and you is he had something to hold onto. But if you die as you are, you have nothing to hold onto and will drop into hell."

This enraged Johnny. He made Mollie stop coming with the children to the meetings. At the school Christmas party he showed his hatred. Mollie asked me what to do. I showed her 1 Corinthians 7:10-16, and instructed her that she must please and follow the Lord. Mollie returned to the assembly fellowship.

Johnny had enough of Mollie's faithfulness. One day he told Mollie he was leaving her. He ordered her to get down and pray with him. She refused because she knew he was just angry. Hypocritically, Johnny flipped open their Bible. He began to read Luke 4 about the temptation of Christ by the devil. God used His word to shine into Johnny's heart and showed him, "That's what you are doing like the devil." Johnny cried out for God's forgiveness and stood up a changed man. So immediate was Johnny's salvation that Mollie did not believe he was saved for another two weeks! He went on for the Lord and never looked back.

During the fall of 1954, Sadie became pregnant with our third child, Barry. During Sadie's expecting period I was always careful to walk with her, especially when slick, icy conditions made walking treacherous. Crossing the little bridge over the creek on the way to our cabin, I took her arm for support. I was paying such care to her that I did not see the little patch of ice in my path. Suddenly in a flash, my feet left me and I skidded to the side of the bridge and underneath it. Sadie was safe and sound up on the bridge, but she was laughing so hard I feared she would lose her footing, too. Both of us had a good laugh at my expense.

One day around that time, a man named Mr. Joy came to visit me. He said I was being an embarrassment to his inter-denominational mission. They did not baptize, break bread, nor conform to several other biblical teachings. Nevertheless, he wanted me to travel out to their mission for once-a-month "missionary Sundays". This he described as their "communion Sunday". He showed no interest as I explained the commission of our Lord. I declined to attend.

He then said that Sadie could not attend "his" doctors in Glenallen for her prenatal care. I objected that we had already prepaid for these doctors' visits. That mattered not to him. As a result, we started going to Palmer for Sadie's check-ups, 225 miles each way, through wintry road conditions and dangerous mountain passes.

After two months of this, Dr. Snyder, one of the two doctors from Glenallen, visited us in Chitina to find out why Sadie had not shown up for her visits. He was shocked to hear the account of Mr. Joy's punitive actions.

"Sadie, you come to my office anytime and you will be treated as one of our own," Dr. Snyder said firmly. "All will be free." Mr. Joy was overruled, and Sadie was treated with Christ-like kindness.

Barry was born in mid-summer on July 1, 1955, in the tiny medical clinic in Glenallen. When it came time to bring Sadie and the baby home, I decided that the evening was the best time to travel because we could open the car vents, equalize the pressure inside the car and thus keep out the road dust. In addition to Sadie, Barry, and I, the car was packed with Sadie's mattress, blankets and various supplies for the new baby. Halfway home, the car's right rear wheel came off the axle. The car dropped awkwardly to the ground.

We were alone, in the middle of nowhere. There really was no other alternative but for me to leave Sadie and the baby in the car while I went for help. I walked five miles to the nearest cabin with mosquitoes and dust my constant companions.

The man at the cabin greeted me rudely. "You're a missionary? Go to hell!" he said and slammed the door.

I walked another mile or so. Hearing the dull rumble of an approaching vehicle, I stopped as my friend Al Taylor brought his old wood-hauling truck to a squeaking stop next to me. Grateful for a friendly face, I asked him for help.

As we drove back to my broken-down car, I told him how the

wheel had come off the axle. "Somebody probably tried to steal your wheel," he said. He figured that someone had loosened the lug nuts but for some reason had not finished the job.

Arriving back at the car, we got the wheel on by a few threads on the studs. Al took Sadie and Barry in his truck, and headed to his cabin. I drove the car very slowly behind them. Just as we reached his cabin, the wheel fell off again. Al and I assessed the situation and determined that there was nothing we could do that night. We would deal with the problem the next day.

Al drove us down the road to an unused cabin where we unloaded Sadie's mattress. We were exhausted, but thankful to have a roof over our heads and a friend helping us along. Even during the long days of July, evenings can get chilly in Alaska. I made a fire in the cabin's stove and put the mattress on the floor in front of the fire. The three of us slept soundly until the morning.

The next day, Al got out the word that we needed a ride back to Chitina. A lady named Barbara drove out and brought us home. Through that contact, she became our friend. Shortly after that, Barbara began coming to the gospel meetings and soon professed salvation. Some years later Al got saved too!

CHAPTER 7

Trials and Triumphs

October 1955
We lived as a family before men, and God used our testimony to confirm our message. It was nice to see natives from far-flung villages come to hear the gospel. A little assembly of 18 believers gathered in the name of our Lord: a church had been planted in Chitina. Of course, Satan would have none of it, and enemies were soon manifesting themselves, often from the most unlikely sources.

The schoolteacher, who professed to be a Christian, accused me of condoning adultery because, according to him, Henry and Etta Bell were not lawfully married. After their salvation, the Bells had become precious followers of Jesus Christ and were in faithful fellowship in the young assembly. The Bells had several children together. According to their Indian tradition, they had appeared before the chief and village council and, upon receiving approval from them, were considered married. I took this as acceptable; but apparently it was not good enough for the schoolteacher.

During a Sunday morning Breaking of Bread service, the teacher walked around outside the meeting and caused confusion. He also wrote to a missionary called Mr. Crabb (whom I did not know) and accused me of condoning sin in the assembly. A couple months later, this missionary and another man came to investigate me. As a courtesy I explained to them my stand that the assembly was autonomous; we were responsible to the

Lord alone and not governed by any outside influence. They seemed reluctant to agree with my conclusions.

The "investigators" stayed for the Breaking of Bread service. Obviously assuming that there would be no standards among the native believers for appearance in the Lord's assembly in such a remote village, they attended the meeting in casual clothes. What a surprise they got when they saw the saints nicely dressed and functioning orderly. I never tried to make the native believers "Irishmen" nor force them into my "foreign" culture; but I never tried to make myself into the native culture, either.

Even though there were doctors in Glenallen, practically speaking they were very far away. As part of our preparations for going to Alaska, a kindly saint in Northern Ireland, Abby Booth, had given me a medical reference book. God enabled me to use homeopathic remedies on several occasions, to good result.

Sadie had mastitis with all the children, and it was no different with Barry. I used medicine according to the book. In three days she was healed. I used homeopathic remedies on several natives and some old prospectors. God used this to open a conversation with these old churlish men. When they wanted to pay, my only charge was that they let me speak to them for ten minutes. Of course I spoke of salvation.

O.A Nelson had boils on his neck and I gave him some medicine that helped. In that way spiritual lessons from earlier years have a way of manifesting themselves in the later lives of reprobates. Nelson wisecracked: "I'm like your friend Job," he said to me. I was not a bit surprised that Nelson knew about the biblical account of Job being covered in boils. Seizing the opportunity, I turned the conversation to the gospel. "Mr. Nelson," I responded. "Job knew the Lord as his Redeemer and worshipped Him. You are not like him because you neither believe on the Lord nor worship Him."

The homoeopathy pills helped him. He had many contests with me, but the Lord always won.

There was the time when O.A. pressured the natives to sign a petition for his liquor license application. Pat Bell came to me to ask forgiveness for his having signed the petition.

"Pat, those who signed the petition were wrong," I said. "How can you pray for your children's salvation yet agree to allow liquor into the village? I can't be with you if you do not get your names removed from that petition."

The thought that he had offended God really rattled Pat. Word got around all the way up to 2nd Chief Goodlataw. The chief personally agreed to go 60 miles to the U.S. Marshal and cancel the native names. I drove him there.

After O.A. found out about this, he went on the warpath and evidently organized men to run me out of town. The native believers were scared and told me to hide. Instead, I decided to face up to him. I walked right up to O.A. and told him he owned almost everything around Chitina and now he could have his own church when I sent to him all the counterfeit Christians who signed his liquor application. He relented and we shook hands. There were no hard feelings in that handshake.

The old bunkhouse was proving to be inadequate for the needs of our family. For one thing, it was very hard to keep warm in winter. The windows would get covered inside with thick frost. When the outside temperatures dipped below zero, the bunkhouse was cold and most uncomfortable. Once time the temperature went down to minus 70 below zero (Fahrenheit) and stayed there for several days. We could hear the nails in the walls literally pop in the wood. This was an urgent situation.

I made plans to build a cabin on a site I selected right next to the church building. Our native friends told us that the best trees for building a cabin could be found about four miles down the frozen Copper River. I set out in the car driving on the river to the place they described.

What a job! It took me most of the morning to cut down, de-limb, and ease that first tree log down the steep slope to the river. My intention was to attach the tree to the car and drag it to the cabin site. But after just one tree I was exhausted.

The next day I used the car to haul two trees at a time. Soon I had figured out how to do the logging operation with greater efficiency, but twenty trees still took the entire day. Through sheer determination and strength from the Lord, I finally I got them all to the site.

I used big, wide trees for the foundation; these were called mudsills. They had to be laid just right on top of the ground. If I dug down and disturbed the permafrost, it would melt and the cabin would sink.

I laboured hard to finish the cabin. O.A came to see what I was doing. "Well, you're not lazy," was all he said before turning and walking away.

A short while later I heard the rumble of a big diesel engine. O.A. was driving his old Caterpillar tractor up the road. Without a word, he started clearing the brush and trees so we could see all around the cabin.

I found an old staircase, some old windows, an old bathtub, (everything was old in Chitina) and several other bits and pieces to put in the cabin. I used old rubber pipes to make plumbing and dug a French drain for drainage. We only had to buy flooring, roofing, tarpaper, nails and a few other things. One of the boys had been given a child-size "Handy Andy" tool kit. Despite their small size, the tools were amazingly well manufactured and I was able to use them for sawing, hammering and assembling the cabin. They don't make toy tools like that today.

All totaled, the cabin cost $110. We still had to get our own drinking water from the creek, but finally we had our own little place and it was very comfortable, too.

Thompsons' Home and Gospel Hall, Chitina, 1955

Our first Christmas in Chitina we were short of funds. Sadie suggested we take the $10 we had and buy something for a Christmas dinner. When I walked through the door of O.A. Nelson's battered old general store, he called out to me, "Thompson, Santa Claus left that box for you." He waved in the direction of a box sitting on the counter.

"Who is the Santa Claus, Mr. Nelson?" I asked. "Just get it the hell out of here," he said.

One of O.A's many roles was that of postmaster. He knew everyone's mail business. He also cashed our checks. Often we only received $10 a month. He knew we had had no Christmas mail.

When I got home and we opened the box, there was ample sufficiency for a good dinner, Tinker Toys for the boys and other goodies. "When a man's ways please the Lord, He makes his enemies to be at peace with him." (Proverbs 16:7) God bent His heart towards us; O.A. was Santa Claus.

> When earth's created streams are dry
> His fullness is the same
> May I with this be satisfied,
> And glory in His Name.

God replaced the adverse teacher. One morning he called for me because he was writhing in pain with some stomach ailment. Thinking he was about to die, he wanted me to forgive him for his actions against our ministry. I assured him that I had forgiven him, but told him that he should seek the Lord's forgiveness. The teacher did not die, but he did move away.

A new teacher and his wife came. They were Christians. One day he gave us a nice, new oil space-heater that they did not need. This was a great blessing because it kept the cabin heated all the time and eased the burden of gathering wood and keeping the fire stoked. The oil space-heater allowed us to visit outlying villages together, assured that the cabin would not freeze while we were gone.

Many other experiences are fondly remembered. After Tom Bell was saved, he taught me how to determine "north" by cutting through a small tree and examining the rings inside its tree trunk. "Where they are narrow, that's north," he instructed me. "It gets no sun in the winter." The knowledge about how to determine north by "reading" a tree got me out of a serious situation once when I got lost coming out of a village.

Tom also showed me how to prepare trees in spring before cutting them down as winter set in. This involved partially cutting around the trunk of the tree. By winter, the prepared trees would be weakened enough to make felling them much easier. I am sure some environmentalists today would frown on such practices, but we were not wasteful and prepared only a select few trees we would need, leaving plenty of others to grow and reproduce.

Sadie made lovely sandwiches for Tom and me that day he was teaching me about preparing trees. I splurged and bought two cans of Coca-Cola. After the trees were prepared, we sat down, gave thanks to the Lord for His provisions and shared the sandwiches for lunch. When I handed Tom a precious can of that rare Coca-Cola, he demurred.

"Too much like old thing!" he exclaimed in broken English. The can of soft drink was too much like the cans of beer he used to consume in excess before he was saved. A paraphrase and new application for Romans 14:21 immediately came to my mind, "....nor Coke whereby thy brother may stumble". I turned around and threw the two cans into the creek. This was a good lesson on Christian liberty taught by Tom. A few days later I retrieved the cans of Coke to share with Sadie and the boys!

* * * * * *

Bathing and washing was always an adventure. We watched the natives and adopted their ideas. We filled a large, empty drum with snow and placed it next to the house heater. The melted snow made especially soft water. Sadie loved the nice soft water for washing her hair. I found a zinc tub for bathing. After everyone had been bathed, the bath water was used for washing clothes. This was a once-a-week chore. When baby Barry arrived, his cloth diapers were washed with the nice soft water. We learned that we could freeze-dry the washed clothes and diapers in the winter by hanging them outside on a clothesline; they froze stiff as boards, but somehow the dampness evaporated!!

As God used the preaching of the gospel to save souls, we were faced with the challenging task of teaching and discipling them. Here again we had much to consider with the differences in culture.

Since the Copper River was too swift and dangerous to use for baptisms, I dammed a little creek for use as baptismal waters. I lined up the new converts on one side bank of the creek. One by one, they would come down to where I would baptize them. Then they would ascend to the other bank of the creek. I used this bank-to-bank exercise as a visual demonstration of what baptism represented.

"When you are on one side, it is like before you were saved you were dead IN sin," I told them. "Jesus died, was buried, and then rose again. When you go under the water, it is a picture of the tomb you are buried in with Him, dead from your old life. Up and out to the other side, you all stand together after you are baptized. That is a picture that shows you are dead TO sin and alive in Jesus Christ." Standing together, sopping wet on the other creek bank, they all understood this step.

The Lord led me to apply other events in their lives to illustrate meeting together and breaking bread in the Saviour's name. I heard Henry Bell tell about a time he and Johnny Billum went moose hunting together. Henry sighted a moose, steadied his rifle and prepared to pull the trigger. Suddenly, even before he pulled the trigger, the moose fell down dead. Johnny had shot the moose from his angle several yards away.

It was a humorous story, but I saw the application in it. I pointed out to the new believers that both Henry and Johnny had the same aim. "When we all have Jesus as our aim," I taught, "We will all come together unto the Lord, but not the moose."

They laughed but understood the concept of Christian unity

right away. What a joy to see for the first time a testimony raised to the Lord's name by these saints in these remote parts of Alaska where Satan had held sway for years. Many precious times were spent like this around the Lord.

Henry got a job over 150 miles away working on a road crew. He came back to Chitina late Saturday nights to be at the Lord's Supper remembrance feast. One time he came, dropped off his wife, Etta, and left.

"Is Henry not coming?" I asked Etta. "No, he's not right," she replied.

I waited for Henry to come back and stopped him. "Henry, why are you not coming in?"

He told me about an argument he had at work. "I said, 'damn you' to the man," Henry confessed.

"Then what did you do?" I inquired. "Well, I said I was sorry."

"What else did you do?" "I asked the Lord to forgive me."

"Did he?" "Yes," Henry answered.

I then explained to him what "unworthy" meant. I asked him to read 1 Corinthians 11:28. "'Let a man examine himself and so let him *stay at home*.' Is that what it says, Henry?" I asked.

"No, Tommy," Henry said, and a smile broke over his face as he realized that fellowship with the Lord and with His saints was the goal of confession and self-examination. Henry had in his past life avoided these problems by getting drunk; now he was learning to face his weaknesses and find strength in the Lord. Henry came into the meeting to remember the Lord and the overflow of his heart in worship brought glory to God.

Another Sunday, Henry had decided he and Etta would go moose hunting. They went out into the woods, but decided to have their devotions before starting their hunt in earnest. That morning they read from Matthew 4:4, "Man shall not live by bread alone." Henry looked at Etta and announced, "We go home, no moose today." They made it in time for the service to remember the Lord. What glorious changes the Lord makes in lives obedient to His word.

* * * * *

Every once in a while, living in a strange culture and experiencing trials of several different kinds, would be discouraging, especially financial challenges. I remember a time when I left Sadie and the children alone to go to visit some villages. I left with a heavy heart. The car broke down - again - in the middle of nowhere.

Frustrated and feeling more than a bit sorry for myself, I cried to the Lord, "Please end my life right here Lord! I just don't know what to do anymore!" It was autumn, so traffic was scarce on that road. Improbably, a small bus came along and stopped. It was full of clean, neatly-dressed, friendly-looking people. They offered me a ride to where I could get help. Delighted, I hopped on board.

As I got to know them, it turned out they were all Mormons. For about an hour I shared the gospel with them. It's a wonder they didn't cast me out like the mariners did with Jonah. Afterwards, it seemed God said, "Get up and go to work and stop feeling sorry for yourself!"

Missionary work has its amusing side. Once I lost my wallet which had two $10 bills inside. The saints prayed and I searched over the places where I had walked, to no avail. Frankly, I was mystified because I really had not gone very far since the last time I remembered having the wallet.

Later that day, I went to the inside "bucket toilet" I had made for family comfort. As I began to sit down, I heard the "plunk" of something falling into the bucket. I quickly looked down into the bucket and saw that the pair of pliers I had in my pocket were now down inside. Well, I didn't know whether to laugh or cry because I knew then where my wallet was, but did not relish the idea of retrieving it. But retrieve it I had to, and did. Sadie and I washed the wallet and the $10 dollar bills, thanking the Lord for helping us find our lost treasure. We were low on groceries and that money was earmarked to fill up our pantry.

I went to O.A. Nelson's general store. Old Clause, the clerk who worked behind the counter, must have suspected something was wrong with the bills. Maybe he heard that sometimes counterfeiters wash money to make it look authentic. I held my breath as Old Clause lifted the two bills up to the light. "These are old," he said with a 'sniff' of authority. "But OK still."

I bought $10.50 worth of groceries, and Old Clause handed me back $9.50 of clean change. When I got home and told Sadie about Old Clause examining those bills, we both laughed to tears. "Old?" Sadie howled with laughter. "I'll say they were old. If only he knew!"

Furthermore, at the assembly prayer meeting when those who had prayed with me asked about the wallet, I told them the whole story. There was too much laughing to do much praying that night.

Another time the native men were bemoaning the fact they had taken no moose that season. I was no hunter, but I knew they tracked moose by looking for hoof prints. One morning when I went to the spring for water, I saw some large prints. I ventured to tell the men that I knew where they could track a moose. Excitedly, I led them with their guns at the ready to the spring.

Proudly I pointed out the prints. 2nd Chief Joe came forward to see. He burst out laughing. Soon the other men looked at the tracks and started laughing, too. That wasn't the reaction I expected.

I must have looked like the village simpleton standing there, pointing at my moose tracks, mouth open in confusion as to why they were laughing so hard. When their laughter finally subsided a bit and they had composed themselves, 2nd Chief Joe put his hand on my shoulder. "Thompson," he said. "These tracks are from low bush moose."

The tracks I thought were moose hoof prints were, in fact, tracks left by snow-shoe rabbits. "Low bush" was a reference to one of two types of cranberries that grow wild in Alaska; high bush cranberries grow on waist-high bushes, and low bush cranberries grow on shrubs low to the ground. The men did get some rabbits that day, but not the moose I had hoped they would find. From then on, those men called rabbits "Thompson's Low Bush Moose."

Times of shortage came often, but the Lord was faithful. Once when our food supply had dwindled to only one potato and a bar of baking chocolate, we were concerned about what to do. I had to go up the hill behind our cabin and cut wood. I took little Billy with me. Hearing a little squeak, I turned and saw a rabbit caught in an old snare. Now, in Northern Ireland, some of us thought of rabbits as vermin or pests, not as food, so both Sadie and I avoided eating rabbit. But looking at that rabbit caught in a snare, Acts 10:13 came to my mind. "Rise, Peter, kill and eat."

Having never killed anything before, I could only think of what was called a "rabbit punch" which I think might be a boxing term. Regardless, I went over and knocked the rabbit on its head and killed it. Then I heard another little squeak. This time I turned around and saw little Billy crying. "Daddy, you killed the wee rabbit," he whimpered.

Now I felt awful. Not knowing what to do with my long-eared prey, I asked a neighbor for help. He took the rabbit and skinned it for us. Sadie bravely cooked our meal using one potato and one rabbit. Gathered around the meal, we bowed as I gave thanks for it.

After we had finished the meal, I looked up at Sadie. I still felt terrible for having killed that poor creature, upsetting Billy in the process, and having to eat something we would have normally found inedible. Sadie looked at her plate, then looked at me and wiggled her nose like a rabbit. I stifled a laugh and reminded her that the Lord gave that rabbit to us.

"Look at your plate, you didn't pick the bones either," she said. "Besides, you did not give grace; you asked the Lord for grace to eat it." Once again Sadie's sense of humor had made our predicament laughable.

On another occasion when we had no money to buy food, I prayed, "Lord, Thou hast promised to supply all our need; and, Lord, if this promise fails, then so does John 3:16!" What a bold type of prayer!

The native people are not prone to give things away, but they are especially conservative with their own money. I had no sooner uttered that prayer when there was a knock on the door. I got up and opened the door to one of our native sisters in Christ. Without saying much - we were becoming used to that - this dear lady handed me a $5 bill. Oh, how small I felt, and how humbled. To think that, even as I prayed, this dear lady was on her way to our cabin with the answer in her hand. Even now it brings tears to my eyes. There is not enough time for me to relate all the many gracious provisions of the Lord.

* * * * *

The Apostle Paul wrote in Romans1:16, "For I am not ashamed

of the gospel of Christ." Paul had seen the gospel's power in many changed lives. In Luke 14:21-24, the Lord also said, "Go out into the streets and lanes...highways and hedges." We were surely in the "hedges" of the world, and God's invitation through the gospel message brought the poor, maimed, halt and blind into His feast of salvation. Just a few of those testimonies of salvation will suffice to show God's power.

Sadie had a girls' sewing/knitting/Bible class on Friday nights. Several of these girls professed Christ as Saviour. When I started holding Sunday school, I tried to use the native people as far as possible. One day, the teacher for one of the older children's classes did not show up. I asked one of the teacher's children where her father was. Her answer showed how much I was ignorant of their culture. "My Dad is away hunting!" the little girl chirped. Provision for food had priority.

While visiting another village, FBI agents were there investigating about goods stolen from the schoolteacher's house which belonged to the Federal government. One of the agents, an anthropologist by training, questioned the teacher about whether he had given things to the natives. The teacher confirmed that he had given things he thought they needed or that he did not need any more.

"That was your mistake," the federal anthropologist told the teacher. "When you give away so much, they think you are being better than them. Allow them to work for any surplus you have. In their potlatch ceremonies they give away many things like blankets, guns, and furs. The longer a potlatch lasts and the more gifts given, the higher the giver rises in the estimation of the tribe."

When I heard that, I then understood why the Lord had sent us to Chitina empty-handed with nothing more to give the people than the gospel. They knew we were not any better than they were, but even came and gave us many things as thanks "for coming and living with us". I cried with joy at "being poor but making many rich".

The devil was active in other ways. Once, a Pentecostal preacher came to view Chitina village. He told O.A. Nelson he could bring lots of money into the community. He wanted to buy land and build a church. O.A. was never one to turn away from making money, but something about that preacher must have rubbed him the wrong way.

"We have our own missionary and he lives by faith," O.A. Nelson told the preacher, referring to me. "We don't need you, so get the hell out of this town."

Old O.A.'s treatment of the man was crude but effective. It gave a new meaning to the proverb, "A house divided against itself cannot stand."

Our boys were badly frightened by an atheistic man known as Alex. He would even verbally abuse Sadie in the general store. "You people can't do anything with these savage Indians," he growled at her. "This God of yours can't do anything about them, either."

He once chased Brian and Billy with a switchblade knife, shouting, "I'll knife you, you wee Jesus boys."

When I heard about that, I lost my patience with him. A few days later I saw him coming down toward his cabin.

"I'll not kill him, Lord," I prayed. "But just let me drop him into the creek with one good punch."

Needless to say, the Lord did not give me permission to take such matters into my own hands, or fists as the case may be. I didn't touch Alex. It wasn't long before he just stopped

59

bothering any of us. That man died cursing God to his last breath.

* * * * *

Then there were the victories. George Brickle was a white man who was married to a very rough Indian woman named Suzie. They lived in a shack of a cabin about a half-mile down the old railway line. I went to visit and found him in a filthy condition, paralyzed by a severe stroke and neglected in every way. His hair covered his face and head like the mane of a lion. His mouth was caked with dried vomit. His speech was slurred.

I spent time with him over the next three days. I spoke of the grace of God and the love of Christ as I cut George's hair, shaved him and generally cleaned him up. I gave him homeopathic tablets. He began uttering words of appreciation. George showed a deep interest in Christ's death for sinners. He told me he was a veteran of both World Wars. He said Suzie intercepted his pensions and used the money to buy liquor, which she drank constantly.

I contacted the military veterans' authorities and explained his condition. An Army helicopter was scheduled to pick him up. When George heard the news, he wept. "I have accepted Jesus for myself now," he said. "I'm saved."

The day of his departure I cleaned and dressed him, and brought him to the village centre. The villagers were amazed to see his transformation. I gave him a big hug and with tears of joy he was taken away by helicopter transport to the military hospital. "Delivered, by the power of God."

John Stanfield was a white prospector who had married an Indian woman nicknamed Blind Fanny. He was a story in himself, but this time he was in trouble. I drove him 220 miles one winter, all the way to the Palmer hospital, because of his bleeding ulcer. The ulcer nearly killed him. It took over two months before I could return to Palmer and bring him back.

John and Blind Fanny lived on the opposite side of Lake Chitina. One night, the noise of a party at their cabin was so pronounced that we could hear it at our cabin. I went over and found a scene of drinking and immorality that was disgusting. I made my way into John's cabin and warned him about his recent near-call with death. I also told the native revelers that God promised judgment on sin. They shouted me down. When one of them raised his hand to strike me, a local Chitina native man stopped him. "Don't hit our missionary," he warned the would-be assailant. Things were heating up.

Just then a big, native man grabbed me by the scruff of my neck and pushed me out the door. I thought about freeing myself (football shins etc) but instead I told him, "Look in the window. God has all that in His book for judgment day and you, too, will be punished for all your sins written down in His book." The big man released his meaty grip, and I ran for home.

Eighteen months later, I was preaching in Mentasta Village many miles away. A car drove up and stopped. A huge man stepped out and approached me. "Do you remember me?" he asked with a smile.

How could I forget the big man who hustled me by the neck out of John's cabin that night?

"You spoke good words to me," he said and introduced himself as Pete Ewan. "I did not go back into the cabin that night," Pete said. "Instead I walked home, 60 miles. On the way I got saved. Now I hold a good job."

The joy on his face and the peacefulness of his demeanor gave evidence of his conversion. Just then a lovely woman and some children emerged from the car. "And this," Pete said, gesturing toward them, "is my wife and kids."

John Stanfield's neighbor, Charlie, had a stroke and I was summoned to help him. It was some time before he was discovered. Charlie's wood stove had gone out and the lower parts of his legs were cold as ice. I used Vick's ointment to rub on the frozen parts, and I tried to get some homeopathic milk pills down his throat. He rallied for a while, but then died.

I dressed Charlie's corpse, made a coffin, put the body in it, and left it in his cabin. As I passed John's cabin, I turned in to speak with him.

"John, do you remember when you nearly died and I had to take you to Palmer?" I asked. "God spared your life then. But, do you remember I told you about how Jesus died for you because of your sins? John, if you had died like Charlie there," and I jerked my thumb in the direction of Charlie's cabin, "You would be in hell for all eternity."

"Golly, Thompson, what must I do?" Obviously John was listening seriously. I did not pour in oil or wine just then, but wanted to press him about his sin. "John, you need to repent of your sins. You need to ask God to forgive you and save you," I said firmly.

Right then, John dropped down at his table and prayed. "God, forgive me and save me." It was just about as simple as that.

He rose up with an expression of what could only be described as a man at peace with God. That same afternoon, John led Blind Fanny to Christ. Their lives from that point forward showed God's power to change.

I went to see O.A. Nelson about burying Charlie's body. "Just leave him up there at his cabin," O.A. replied. "He won't go anywhere." I told him Charlie was some mother's son and burial arrangements needed to be made. O.A. just waved me away. Days after that, old 'friends' entered Charlie's cabin and carried away his possessions. I tried to stop this until I learned it was a custom among the old prospectors.

When John and Blind Fanny were baptized that summer, some of John's old friends taunted him by calling out, "What will John do now for his bottle?"

Once Fanny was told in sympathy, "It must be hard to be in darkness all the time." "It's not dark," she quietly responded. "I have the Light of Jesus all the time."

When Thomas Pete got drunk, he was a wild man. One time in a drunken rage, he tried to break down Suzie's cabin door. Never one to rely on anyone else for help, Suzie calmly pulled out her rifle, drew a bead on the intruder and shot off Thomas Pete's leg. He was evacuated to a hospital and returned with a prosthetic leg.

According to the variegated and often conflicting roles of firearms to the way of life in an Alaskan village, Suzie made amends with Thomas Pete by presenting him with a rifle. It was almost 18 months before a U.S. Marshal came to investigate the shooting and so far as I know nothing ever came of the investigation. "Suzie, why did you shoot Thomas?" "I prayed to God and He told me to shoot but shoot low!" The Marshall let her go with a smirk and he left too. Later, Thomas Pete came to the gospel meeting and was saved. When I baptized him, he was one of eleven baptized at the same time.

Little Robert was only about 10 years old when he started coming to the gospel meetings. He had a sad, impoverished home life. His mother was an alcoholic and often left him to fend for himself. Many times she was not home at all. He started coming to the gospel meetings because it was warm in the hall in the wintertime. He listened well.

One night, little Robert went to his Uncle Joe and said he wanted to be saved. Joe led him to Christ. At the meeting the next night he sang the hymns enthusiastically with a new heart. I was not surprised when afterwards he told me he was saved the previous night.

When summer came, the fine silt surface of the roads in Chitina turned to deep dust in some places. Little Robert was playing with some children. Somehow, he hit his head and fell face-first into the dusty road. The dust curled up and acted like a suffocating agent in the nose, throat and lungs of the lad. I was called to help. For hours we gave him artificial respiration. But little Robert had choked to death. I carried his lifeless body to the Gospel Hall. I made a child-sized coffin and dressed him nicely.

At the funeral, little Robert's mother came, drunk as usual, and made a terrible fuss. Life for Robert was never easy, neither was his death. We took some solace knowing that he would enjoy peace, care and life everlasting in the arms of his heavenly Father. Several years later, little Robert's alcoholic mother got saved and her life showed it too.

Axel Ring was the son of the shaman, Ring Charlie, who had died. I visited Axel when he was sick and spoke about his soul's salvation. He diagnosed himself as a hopeless case before God. "Me big sinner," he said.

As if by way of proving the enormity of his sin, he told some disturbing things he had done to people. After he told me many things, I had to admit to him that any one of those things was enough to send him to hell. "But, I like to be saved," he said, pleadingly.

Pointing to his medicine tablets and glass of water next to his bed, I asked him what they were for. "Make me better," he answered.

"How, Axel?" I countered. He pantomimed putting a tablet in his mouth, washing it down with a drink of water, and its effects being disbursed through his body to bring relief.

Then I turned to Romans 10:8-11. Slowly, using his own illustration of taking his medicine, I explained how to be saved. "Axel, with your mouth, confess," I said, "but swallow in your heart for it's with your heart you trust." Then God says, 'Saved.'"

I left him to visit some others. Upon my return, a peaceful radiance was on Axel's face. He welcomed me with a smile. "Me now saved," he said.

Many years later when Malcolm Radcliffe and I had gospel meetings in Anchorage, Axel's granddaughter was saved. They have four children and still live in Chitina. We visit them when we can.

CHAPTER 8

Beyond Chitina

Using Chitina as our center of operations, we reached out to other villages. Tetlin was about 150 miles away on one of two reservations in Alaska. We had to drive to the Alaska Highway, and then hire a bush pilot to fly us to the village. Jimmy Henry, who was saved many years before through Harold Richards' preaching, lived in this village. It was Jimmy who wrote and invited us to come.

Peter Joe, the village chief, greeted us warmly. "You are welcome," Chief Peter said. "I am happy you are bringing church to my people."

He opened his cabin for gospel meetings and allowed us to sleep in the cabin belonging to the Episcopalian bishop. We had Bible school every day with the children. During the gospel meetings the people gave good attention. A few professed salvation.

The chief came during the day and we had long talks. He would tell the story of his people as far back as 400 years, and it was most interesting. I told him my story of the Son of God and His love in coming to die for our sins. I used imagery he could relate to, such as "trail" instead of "the way." One day Chief Peter declared, "I'm on the right trail now!"

He seemed to have a grasp of the gospel of Christ and I feel certain he got saved. In subsequent visits to Tetlin, Chief Peter showed he was truly saved.

Once I noticed he only brought in one log at a time to burn in his heating stove. "Why do you bring in only one log for heat at a time?" I asked. "I have to stack up many logs for my wife to use."

"Only need one, for I might die," was his answer. "But, if you die, what will your wife do?" I wanted to know. "Oh, she can get her own," he said with a smile. I laughed. That would have never done with my Sadie.

Chief and Mrs Peter Joe, 1956

When the Lord works, the devil is busy trying to hinder. But many times, those who are supposed to be Christian workers put up enough roadblocks and engage in turf wars over the gospel so that all Satan has to do is sit back and watch.

School was out early, so I had children's meetings each day

and gave them memory verses to learn. The bishop wrote me forbidding me to enter 'his' area again. I wrote back suggesting that he should be ashamed to admit being in that area for so long yet even the chief was not saved, but now he and others were.

Another time, I arrived and the first cabin I visited belonged to Alfred. He looked sad. I asked him what the matter was. "We have all fallen out of the nest," Alfred said, glumly. He meant that there were many villagers who lost their salvation.

Further inquiry revealed that a Pentecostal preacher went into Tetlin, again. He had sowed seeds of doubt in their minds. I opened my Bible to Hebrews 7:25 and asked Alfred to read it.

"Who is able to save?" I asked Alfred. "God," he said, looking at the passage.

"Do you know what 'uttermost' means?" I asked. I explained that it means salvation is assured right up into heaven. The joy returned to Alfred and others who were saved but had been discouraged. I heard that Alfred would tell others about being "saved to the utmost."

We made many visits to Tetlin. One winter Harold Richards and I were there. We got news that our airplane could not come to pick us up. We decided to walk the 14 miles out to the Alaska Highway. Jimmy Henry went out the night before and we were to follow his dog-sled tracks. He left a good trail, even breaking branches at points where the trail divided so we would know which path to take. We made good time. Harold and I took turns in the lead and that seemed to help our progress.

Coming to the river, Jimmy's sled tracks appeared to cross over it. Unknown to us the river was open along its edges. Gingerly,

Harold stepped on the frozen river. He hadn't taken more than a couple steps on the ice when it gave way and he sunk up to his knees in the icy water. I was close enough to pull him out before he went any further in, but his lower legs were soaking wet.

We prayed for the Lord's help. "Lord, you took the Israelites over the Red Sea and the Jordan," I prayed aloud. "When we find a safe place to cross, give me the peace (Col 3:15) of assurance in my heart."

Harold followed like one of the mixed multitude. I cut down a tree branch for testing the ice. We traveled quite a way downriver when I finely felt assured we could cross at a certain spot. With my rod-of-Moses tree branch, I tapped and walked, carefully but with faith, out onto the frozen river. About halfway across, I turned around to check on Harold. He wasn't behind me. I looked in the distance and saw him on the river bank, looking anxious.

"That is scriptural, too, Harold," I shouted. "The Israelites stood still on the banks of the Jordan, but God brought them over. Come with me, because the Lord told me to cross here."

With concern painted across his face, Harold took a deep breath and crossed over in my footprints. We both made it across, safely this time. But then we had to make our way back upriver to catch up with Jimmy's tracks from the night before. With no path outlined "we walked by faith". It was a difficult trek. Finally, we came to Jimmy's tracks.

We were both physically spent; Harold especially so. We hiked on. We arrived at Midway Lake. As we started crossing over the frozen lake, we began to feel very tired and sleepy. This was a sign that hypothermia was setting in. I foolishly took out some prunes and ate them with snow. This was like throwing cold water on a fire because the energy consumed by my mouth to melt the snow actually decreased my body temperature.

We couldn't walk more than a few yards at a time before feeling compelled to sit and rest. As we rested, we felt like falling asleep. We were in a very dangerous and potentially perilous condition. We were sitting by the trail dozing off again, when I felt someone shaking me awake.

"Thompson, wake up! Brother Richards, wake up!" It was Jimmy Henry. He had been on his dog sled looking for us all day. When he saw us, he came and loaded us both on his sled and his powerful dog-team pulled us to his cabin. Before long we were wrapped in blankets sitting by the roaring stove in his cozy cabin, drinking hot tea while our wet clothes dried. I could not help but praise God who had saved Jimmy's soul and then used Jimmy to save our lives. But not only that, Jimmy gave us a gift of $5 out of his earnings from his fur trap-line.

I have spoken before of the interference we received from those who were ostensibly supposed to be helping the local population. It happened in Tetlin, too. Once in late autumn, the village schoolteacher scheduled a movie to be shown at the same time as our previously-scheduled gospel meeting. We decided to go, too. The machine would not work. We all waited for quite a while as he fussed and fidgeted with the movie projector, trying to fix it. Finally, I told him, "This machine will not work." I announced that we could all go over to Chief Peter's house for a gospel meeting.

During this same visit, I went to see a native family. Inside their cabin, the young daughter had open sores nearly three inches in diameter. My heart went out to her. I sought out the schoolteacher who, as the U.S. government representative, had access to information and resources that might bring some relief to the sick family. I wondered whether it would expedite things if we flew the child out with us for medical care.

"Leave her alone," the teacher said rather gruffly. "Her father died with tuberculosis and so will she."

I went to Chief Peter with my idea to evacuate the little girl. He had no problem giving me permission. In spite of the teacher's antics, I asked him to fly the mother and sick little girl out to the highway. He grudgingly agreed to do so. On his return, I asked him to take us out, too. After he had taken off with us inside, he turned around and, over the noise of the engine, said, "New winter rates today!"

He charged us double the price. I warned him that the money we used was really the Lord's money, but he didn't seem fazed by that. We paid the double fare and he flew us to the highway. The good news was that the sick little girl got the help she needed.

Unfortunately, after the schoolteacher returned to the village, after leaving us at the highway, he crashed his airplane and was forced to make some very expensive repairs. Can a man rob God? The schoolteacher found out that the answer is "no".

The Indians had dogsled races in the winter. I would go to the races and conduct gospel meetings at night afterwards inside cabins. We had some good meetings. I slept in a tent and used a Yukon Stove for heat. Taking another lesson from the native ways, I weaved evergreen branches like a carpet and put them on the floor. It was almost comfortable.

Mentasta Lake was another village in which I ministered. In 1955, Sadie, the children and I made our first visit there and were received kindly. This village was 200 miles from Chitina and six miles from the main road.

We started off conducting gospel meetings in Katie John's cabin. As a mother and grandmother, Katie John was a well-respected village elder. The meetings were very well attended - too well, in fact. I soon saw that we needed a better place to have meetings.

I made a proposal to the village men. If they would harvest the logs - easy for them to get - I would supply everything else and we would build a combination schoolhouse-Gospel Hall. The natives were thrilled with the prospect of a school in the village. Like all cultures, Alaska natives love their children. Until then, the Mentasta Lake children had to leave home and attend a centralized school for that area. As the children entered high school, they had to go as far away as southeastern Alaska.

I approached the territorial government's educational authorities with the proposal. Since there were more that 10 children in the village, they agreed to a school. A teacher whom I led to the Lord had a current teaching certificate. He gladly went to teach. So, it was not long before the proposed building took shape and became a reality.

It was a good building and quite warm in the winter, too. We bought an old trailer and placed it next to the building to stay in when we visited. God blessed even further when the government authorities said they would pay us $400 per month to rent the school. I turned over this income to the village leaders to be used for their needs.

God worked in the salvation of several women, including Katie John. Some men were saved, too.

One day before eating my lunch I went for a brisk walk. It was 30 degrees below zero. Suddenly, a little girl ran out of her cabin with her clothes ablaze. Apparently in an effort to get warm, she had gone too close to the stove and her clothes caught fire. I immediately rolled her in the snow and extinguished the flames.

I remembered that earlier some men had been drinking tea from a pail. I rushed and grabbed the pail, steeped a pair of long-john underwear in the tea, and wrapped the girl inside the long-johns. I called out to the men to get one of their trucks started, not quickly or easily done in sub-zero temperatures. Katie John held the child and I marshaled the men to climb on the truck with shovels. It had snowed about 10 inches since the last time the road was cleared. When the truck got stuck in the snow, the men got out and cleared the way.

We reached the main road six miles away and went into Mentasta Lodge. I phoned Dr. Pinneo in Glenallen and he agreed to meet us at Chistochina Lodge further down the road. We made good time, except a large moose lumbered across the road and we missed it by inches. At Chistochina Lodge, the lodge owner kept her electric blanket turned on all day. She let us use her private, warm bedroom. It was only minutes before Dr. Pinneo and a nurse from a Christian mission came. I hugged them as they took over.

After examining the injured girl and administering some palliative measures, the doctor made contact with the U.S. Army. They were having winter training near that area. The Army mobilized a helicopter to the lodge and flew the child to Anchorage. By 6 p.m. that same evening, the little burn victim was in good hands.

When we finally returned to Mentasta Village, I conducted a gospel meeting. A man and his wife were saved. After I finally climbed into bed, I could not stop crying tears that were a mixture of relief and praise to the Lord.

On another of my visits to Mentasta Lake, I went to see some natives who had set up a camp while they were trapping for muskrats. One of them, Oscar, an elderly Christian man, told me he would come to the gospel meetings. "I come," he said, "after I visit my trap lines."

I asked him if I would be bringing his wife to the gospel meeting. "I don't know, Thompson," he said. "She don't hear good."

After Oscar went off to check on his trap line, I went to his cabin to introduce myself to his wife. As I spoke to her, I was surprised to find that she seemed to hear me just fine. I invited her to the gospel meeting and she came.

Later, I told Oscar that, contrary to what he told me, his wife did not seem to have any hearing problem that I could discern. Oscar responded by quoting John 5:24. "'He that hears my word, and believes on him that sent me, has everlasting life,'" Oscar said. "You see? My wife, she don't hear good!" I laughed and finally understood. Oscar meant that his wife was not saved.

CHAPTER 9

Children's Camps

Sadie and I went down to some of the fish camps that the Natives set up near the rivers during the summer to catch fish for their families and dogs. This was a busy time for the villagers as they worked hard during the long summer days to provide subsistence for the winter. We got the idea that we could have meetings for the children during the day, and then gospel meetings at night for the adults. This worked out fine. From this the Lord exercised our hearts to have a camp for the children from all the villages. For $15, I purchased an acre of land with an old cabin on it in Lower Tonsina. We repaired the cabin, and we cleared the land of rubbish with help from some of the children from Chitina.

As I was digging a latrine, my shovel hit permafrost with such force that I fell over the hole. This accident resulted in a severe back strain that put me out of commission once again. (I had hurt my back in 1953 in Cape Town working for the oil company. It gave me lots of pain and trouble. It was also hurt in Belfast when we were on our way to Alaska.)

I was put in traction for two weeks. Two one-gallon cans filled with gravel were attached to my medical corset with ropes and thrown over the elevated foot of the bed. This all cost me valuable time.

When I felt better I went to the doctor in Glenallen, and he adjusted my back. "Don't lift anything heavier than a pencil," the doctor advised.

I, however, went down to Anchorage to buy supplies for the camp. The Army was revamping nearby Fort Richardson Army Post and was auctioning off surplus equipment. I made a bid on three tents: one 14 x 16ft, one 16 x 24 ft, and one 10 x 12 ft. My bid of $50 was accepted. Once again, God not only met our expectations, He exceeded them! What I did not know was that all the equipment under the tents went with the bid. There were steel beds and mattresses, metal tables, a steel sink, serving trays and many things that seemed custom-ordered for our new children's camp.

Harold Richards loaned me his big truck. We transported the whole load back to the Lower Tonsina campground. Harold helped me set up tents. There were enough logs available to erect a dining room addition to the old cabin.

The territorial government authorities asked me whether they could use our facility in the event of an emergency. This was the middle of the Cold War between the Soviet Union and the United States. This kind of request was not unusual, given Alaska's strategic global location. At a certain point, Alaska is only two miles from Siberia. We agreed to the government's request. This enabled us to get food surpluses and a motor boat, too.

Children came to our camp from as far as 200 miles away. During my visits to villages, the children were given memory verses to learn. During subsequent visits, children who knew their memory verses were rewarded with free admission to the camp. I never knew of one child who could not repeat their memory verses with this incentive!

More than 80 children enrolled the first season. We transported many of them from their villages and returned them home again. At the camp, the children could earn tokens for doing various things, especially for giving correct answers after the Bible lessons. All these things won their cooperation and respect.

After lunch was a "compulsory rest period" (everything was a quiet as a mouse), and the children could spend their tokens at a little "store" we opened. The rest periods benefited everyone; the workers were glad of a wee rest, too. There was a "good sleeper" award, and some children even had to be wakened up!

We inspected the children's hands and faces for cleanliness as they filed into the dining cabin. This exercise provided us with some hard-to-suppress chuckles. I pointed to one little boy's dirty neck and instructed him to go clean it. He left. Soon he came through the line again. When I inspected his neck, that one little spot where my finger had touched gleamed like an island of cleanliness in a sea of dirt. I made my instructions much more specific the second time around.

We also provided the children with clean underwear donated by the Valley Christian Children's Home. We handed out the underwear after administering baths. For this we used two big Army-issue bread-mixing bowls, each about 36 inches in diameter. We used one bowl for washing them, and the other to rinse them. I channeled a nearby creek to the camp, so there was plenty of water. Workers and children alike had many good laughs when our soapy charges slid out of the bowls.

Native children in those days mostly wore handmade moccasins: slipper-type footwear made from animal skins, lined inside with rabbit fur. Since each child's moccasins were custom-made just for them, each pair was unique and easily identified. One of the children's favorite games was when we mixed up their moccasins in a pile. After we said "go" the children would race to the pile and scramble to find their own moccasins. The first ones back to the starting line with both of their own moccasins on would win tokens.

We taught Scripture lessons regularly. We also had gospel meetings for parents who came in from their fish camps. Quite a number of adults attended each evening. One boy wanted to be saved and actually Billy my son led him to the Lord. The next day the boy spoke to me and said, "Now I want to be a Christian!" He soon was instructed in the way of God more perfectly.

Bible Camp, 1957

A crew of student surveyors was working nearby and we invited them to the meetings, too. They all came, probably motivated by curiosity. I visited the survey crew as they worked toward Chitina. Sadie and I invited them over to our home after Sunday evening gospel meetings. They gobbled up Sadie's delicious homemade treats. They hadn't had home cooking for months. We were able to speak to them about the things of God and they were receptive to our message.

After the survey crew had finished their projects and gone back to their homes in the Lower 48, we received a letter from one of them, Wayne Sparks. I still have a treasured copy of that letter in my study. He described how our ministry had led to his restoration to the Lord. He vowed to serve the Lord from then on. He had enclosed a gift of $20. Wayne wrote to us a few more times after that. Another young man named McMahon wrote and told us he got saved on the plane taking him home to Seattle.

Helpers in the children's camp were a good team: Etta Bell, Mollie Billum, Paul and Edna Hammon, Ethel Zinn, Sadie and me. Over the following years, we had some others who came and helped. It was a big undertaking, but it was motivated by devoted love. We felt it was the same kind of love Mary Magdalene showed after Jesus Christ's death when she went to the authorities and said, "Tell me where you have laid Him and I will take Him away". Although a weak vessel, she was ready to carry the body of the Lord.

Devotion to the Lord Jesus Christ is the secret of serving. As the hymn writer put it,

> *I would not work my soul to save,*
> *For that my Lord has done;*
> *But I would work like any slave*
> *For love of God's dear Son.*

The Lord always met the need of the children's camp work for all the years we did it. Even after we moved to Anchorage, we still carried on this work each summer.

Over the years I have met people from these places where we spent our early years. I had a Sunday Bible Class for children at the Alaska Native Hospital in Anchorage. One evening, I met a young man named Tom Titus. He was from Tetlin. He was dying with cancer, and he had already had one leg amputated. I talked to Tom about my ministry in his home village and about the camp we had.

"Tom," I said to him, "When I leave you tonight I could die and would go to Heaven. But then we would never see each other again. If you died first where would you go?" "I would go to heaven, too," he replied. "How can you be sure?" I pressed.

He then related that after one Bible Class he asked the Lord to "forgive me my sins and save me". Tom will be united in heaven with his forbears from Tetlin who were saved by the grace of God.

Another time, years after leaving Chitina, I went into the restaurant at Summit Lodge, off the highway in Alaska. I recognized one man's face and I went over to him.

"Did you ever go to a Sunday School in Anchorage?" I asked. The man turned to me and smiled with recognition. "Yes, Uncle Tommy," he said. "I'm saved, and also my wife. We go to a church near our home."

CHAPTER 10

Wasilla

One by one, family by family, the believers from Chitina were moving to Anchorage. The village school closed. We began sensing the Lord preparing us for a different work.

About that time, we were invited to move to Wasilla where the Valley Christian Children's home was operated by Harold and Mabel Richards. Wasilla was little more than a dot on a map about 45 miles north of Anchorage, a far cry from the busy town of thousands of people today. The Richards cleaned out and remodeled an unused chicken coop, and we moved into it to await the Lord's leading and for Brian to go to school.

We enjoyed helping out at the children's home, and I became a member of its board of directors. It was a good work which the Richards originally started in their home in the southeast Alaskan community of Cordova; they had also planted a new assembly of believers in Cordova. The Richards were the first assembly missionaries to Alaska who had stayed for any significant length of time.

Their work in Cordova was transferred to Wasilla in the Matanuska Valley. The Matanuska Valley has rich soil and good conditions for farming. The U.S. government had offered subsidies to entice farmers to move there and establish dairy farms and raise crops. This is where the world-famous giant cabbages are grown. A number of these "colonists" from the

Midwestern United States had moved there about 1935. Land was easy to buy, and soon, with lots of hard work, the Valley Christian Children's Home was established.

Harold's widowed sister, Ethel Zinn, whom everyone lovingly referred to as Aunt Ethel, had retired from school teaching. At an age when other people think of resting, she moved to Alaska to help in this work. I will ever appreciate these dear saints, all of whom have now entered the presence of the Lord whom they served very faithfully.

I was asked to speak at a gathering of the six other Christian homes in the area. My text was 1 Corinthians 4:15. "Though ye have ten thousand instructors in Christ, yet have ye not many fathers: for in Christ Jesus I have begotten you through the gospel."

My message was entitled "Pedagogue", and its purpose was to encourage the children's workers to see that one day their work would bear fruit. In a passing reference, I mentioned their own personal need to keep in communion with the Lord for spiritual growth. I said they should not think that a little church sermon on Sunday was sufficient because otherwise they would never mature and preachers would become like spiritual baby sitters. Little did I know that some "reverends" were in the audience and they were not pleased. Apparently, they went back and warned their "flock" about me.

However, John Martin, a businessman, enjoyed the message and came and told me so. "When you move to Anchorage," he said to me, "I have a piece of property you will need and you can have it very reasonably." We had not told anyone of our exercise about moving to Anchorage. "Who told you I would move to Anchorage?" I asked. He just smiled and said, "Oh, I just figured you would go there."

CHAPTER 11

Anchorage

Anchorage sprang up in 1915 first as a tent city around a landing at the mouth of Ship Creek. The federal government had selected the site for the headquarters for the construction of the Alaska Railroad. It was no sooner founded when suddenly there was a population of 2,000 people. Anchorage has been an expanding boomtown ever since.

By the beginning of the 1960s, defence spending to develop Elmendorf Air Force Base and Fort Richardson Army Post had caused the population to grow exponentially: more than 40,000 people had moved to Anchorage over the previous two decades. The greater metropolitan population today approaches 300,000 people, nearly half the population of the entire state. Anchorage has been the largest city in Alaska since the late 1940s.

Anchorage's population is cosmopolitan. It has always acted like it was a city three or four times its actual size. However, since its economy is based on the military, and industries like fishing, oil, and tourism, it is a very transient place and this made for instability even in the Lord's work.

When we moved to Anchorage, at first we rented a small cabin and started reaching out to the community with the gospel message. True to his word, John Martin helped us get the piece of land on which we later made our home.

"I know that you live by faith," he said. I had never told him anything about my support. "Whatever the Lord gives you as a deposit on the land, I'll accept."

I saved up $100 dollars and he gladly took this. The Lord enabled us to pay him the remainder within a year. Being familiar with the Army surplus operation, I purchased a quarter of a surplus wooden building from a man who bought a whole H-shaped building with heating and plumbing in the center. I bought the 20 x 14 ft bare piece that he cut off the end, no windows, doors, or insulation just an empty shell. I got it moved onto our property for $150. It was with gusto we worked on this project and soon the building was livable, but without water or sewage. We made do in ways we had learned while living in Chitina.

Of course, money was tight. We committed our needs to the Lord. I still drove up to the Alaska interior to visit the villages with the gospel. On one trip on my way back, the fuel gauge in my car displayed "empty." I prayed to the Lord to get me home, which he did. Sadie met me with a big smile. "Guess what's in this letter?" she asked, waving an envelope back and forth in her hand. "I don't know," I said, taking the letter to read it.

A certain Mr. Champ from Canada had sent a gift of $400, an enormous sum especially in those days. In the accompanying letter, he wrote about having heard about us, but none of the resources for communicating funds knew us or listed our address. Mr. Champ had persevered for several weeks until he learned where we were and he sent the gift "hoping it would meet your needs".

Meet our needs it did. We installed windows and siding for the outside of the house, (both essential in Alaska winter climate). We were able to put in a floor oil-heater. This we felt made the house more respectable looking to invite people to Gospel meetings.

I started to dig a well for water in our front yard. It proved tough going because of 'hardpan' so I had dug only waist deep in half a day! It was nearly as hard as cutting logs for our cabin in Chitina!

John Henry Graham, our neighbour who owned some apartments next door to our house, came and asked me what I was doing digging in my yard. When I told him, he laughed and said, "Just dig under my apartments and hook into the water system." His well was 75 feet deep with really good water. I was so happy to do so. I made a watertight wooden box of planks wrapped in plastic, and insulation with a thaw wire around the copper pipe. Soon we had water in the house. From then on, whenever we used the water even for a cup to drink, we thanked the Lord who had provided an Elim indeed.

I also dug a sewer system in the back garden, making first a large 9 x 9 ft hole 12 ft deep. I then cut logs 9 ft long and made a cess pool and lowered this into the hole. Then I made a ditch for the sewer pipe and all was ready to have a flush toilet. I went over and brought the old bathtub from the Chitina cabin. I found some used plumbing parts at an old abandoned Air Force base building up in Tok area. When I went to pay John Henry each month, he told me to keep the money. "The water costs me nothing," he said. "Use as much as you need!"

When natural gas was made available in the city, many people switched to using it instead of oil for heating. A man called Gene owned a trailer park and converted everything there over to natural gas. While I was picking up his daughter for Sunday School one morning, Gene approached my car. "Do you have any use for my old water boiler?" he asked. I accepted the whole unit and hauled it to our house. My experience in past jobs came in handy and I was able to install the boiler. I gathered some old pipes from a disused Army barracks. Soon I had the

Toil and Treasure in Alaska

boiler supplying hot water heating throughout the whole house. It also supplied hot water through the faucets for cooking, bathing, dish washing and such things. How good is the God we adore!

Having shepherded the Indian saints after they left Chitina, I gathered those who lived in Anchorage and began with gospel meetings in our home. The Lord blessed and we saw souls saved. I then felt free to gather the saints who had come from Chitina, and we also began the Breaking of Bread and all the other services in our home. Greatness is not the place or numbers but the presence of the Lord in the midst (Matthew18:20). The Lord blessed increasingly.

Needing more room for visitors I approached the American Legion about use of their large hall. They granted permission to use it on Sundays from 6 am. to 2 pm. Going from door to door with invitations to Bible Class and Sunday School the attendance increased, with some parents attending. We continued using the American Legion hall and our home for the assembly meetings until we built our own Gospel Hall.

As door-to-door visitation continued, the witness became better known. All the believers in the assembly began reaching out, too. A girl named Rebecca became our first convert - she was brought by Alice Billum, a Chitina believer. Everyone worked together and soon young men from the Army & Air Force bases began attending.

Air Force Sergeant Robert "Bob" Denyer and his wife Esther were a special blessing to the assembly. They put their hearts into the work. Bob was treasurer and cleaned the Gospel Hall; Esther was an excellent young children's Sunday School teacher.

On Friday nights, we went downtown and conducted open-air gospel meetings after having the children's meeting. We preached to crowds of people who were there to "cruise the bars and have a good time" as they called it. One night a big man lumbered up to me as I preached and swung his fist at me. "Shut up!" he bellowed. I neatly ducked under his arm and kept on preaching, using him as an example of the type of people God's grace can save. Well, this enraged the big man. But, suddenly, another man intervened and warned the big man to leave. With barely a murmur, the big man spun on his heel and disappeared. So did the other man. I have wondered since if the other man was an angel. Perhaps!

Happy days of fellowship were blessed by the Lord with a good number of souls being saved. Psalm133:1 says, "Behold, how good and how pleasant it is for brethren to dwell together in unity." Unity of saints commands a blessing by the Lord.

We needed a place more convenient for the assembly work that was taking place. I heard about a suitable piece of property located near the intersection of Northern Lights Boulevard and C Street, just a couple blocks from our house.

When passing through Chigago, Mr Bill McCartney, an Ulster man who founded the Stewards' Foundation, told me they would help with a building if needed. Application for their help was made to Bill, and it was graciously granted. The Lord enabled us to repay the loan in a short time.

I made a bid for a surplus Army building, but lost the bid by a slender margin. In a way, we were relieved because we really did not have the money in hand to cover the bid. We were a bit mystified about God's timing when, just a day after we lost the bid, we received a significant monetary gift that would have more than covered it. Then two days after the bids closed, we got a call from the Army. "Mr. Thompson," the officer said, "We apologize for the mistake. You actually won the bid. Your bid was $6 above the other bid." Faith was honored by the Lord. That two-day "lapse" was a mystery no longer. Now we had the money to not only cover our bid, but enough to pay for moving the old surplus motor workshop to our lot on Blueberry and Northern Lights Boulevard.

Bob Denyer was allowed by the Airforce to have leave for non-profit work. He and I worked day and night with help from some of the other saints when they had time. The assembly soon moved into an attractive Gospel Hall. Our young Billy and Brian did what they could. Bob Denyer and I made a good team on a number of projects. In his spare time Paul Hammon contributed his skills as a carpenter. Without a doubt, the Lord was working in and through His assembly.

We continued to have a good response to our door-to-door outreach efforts, most of the time. Knocking at a door just three houses from the Hall, a man opened the door and aimed a gun at my face. His face was ugly with hate: "Getaway from my door or I'll shoot you." I was frozen with shock at first, but God delivered me, one shaken preacher!

The Lord saved a good number of people from all kinds of ethnic backgrounds. One was Dick Washington. Dick, who is black, was born and raised in College Station, Texas. As a young man, he and his cousin drove to Alaska to seek their fortunes. He found his fortune by opening one of the first dry cleaning businesses in Anchorage. He called it Peacock Cleaners. Its motto was "The cleaner with a thousand eyes". By the early 1960s, Dick was making good money and was a popular person. He drove a big expensive white car. He smoked cigars and was "a real man about town". The Washington children began attending our children's meetings. Dick's wife, Ethel, started coming, too. She would say, "Pray for my Richard." She was saved as a 16 year old girl. Soon she came into fellowship.

I tried to visit Dick, but had no success in getting an audience with him. Then I learned that on Thursday evenings Dick climbed into bed early with a half-gallon of ice cream and a big cigar, and settled in to watch "Gun-smoke" on the television. I timed my arrival just as his TV program started.

"Is your Daddy at home?" I asked when his daughter Jackie answered the door. "Yes," she exclaimed, excited to see me. "But he is in bed!" I went into his bedroom and there he was, nestled in for his entertainment. I deliberately positioned myself between him and the TV set. As he leaned from side to side to get a clear view past me, I just kept moving between him and the screen. "Mr. Washington, I know you are a man of your word, and I don't want to stop you from enjoying 'Gun-smoke,'" I said to him. "So, I'll be going if you promise to come to the gospel meeting on Sunday night to hear Gordon Reager and me preaching." Well, needless to say, Dick quickly promised to come to the meeting. I left him to enjoy his show. I don't think I was in his bedroom more than just a couple minutes.

Dick did attend, just as he promised. And he came back the next night to hear more. As he was leaving the gospel meeting, he shook my hand, looking me square in the eye and saying, "Tommy, I have done what you guys said." Dick Washington had been saved. This turn of events was hard for Ethel to believe. You see, her husband was quite a man-about-town, and she was going to watch carefully to see if his conversion was true. Usually each morning Dick arranged four cigars in his breast pocket before he went over to his dry cleaning operation. The morning after he got saved, he went to work and left the cigars behind. Ethel brought them over to him at work. "Ethel, I don't need them anymore," he told her. "I'm saved."

Since then, Dick Washington has become one of the most respected, faithful and well-loved brothers in the assembly. He never misses a meeting. Well into his 80s, he still runs Peacock Dry Cleaners and works from 6 am. to 8 pm. daily, except on Wednesdays when at 7:30 pm. he arrives for the Bible Reading and Prayer Meeting.

Another outstanding conversion was Joe Eskilada, one of the men I first met in the bottle-strewn abandoned rail car in Chitina. He got hurt in a car accident and was brought into the Alaska Native Hospital in Anchorage. With no chance to drink alcohol, Joe sobered up to the point where I could visit and speak to him about the provision God made for him in Christ, His Son, who died that we may live.

After Joe was discharged from the hospital, he came to the Anchorage meetings faithfully with his sister Hattie Mack who was also from Chitina and a dear sweet child of God. A young airman named Wally had recently got assurance of salvation while attending Gospel meetings I shared with Leonard Mullan, missionary to Japan. After one meeting Wally turned to Joe and asked, "Are you saved?" The weight of conviction became too much for Joe, and he broke down and cried out for God to save him. Joe became a faithful follower of Jesus Christ. I got him a job with a Christian builder named Carl Rylander. "I wish I had ten Joes," Carl told me one day. "He is such a good worker."

Many others were saved whose stories thrill my soul. Through circumstances, Master Sergeant Milton Rowcroft was appointed by a military chaplain to teach a Sunday School class. Milton was ignorant of any truth. His wife, who had been saved through our preaching, told him she could get a man to help him and called on me. "Don't try to teach me that Jesus is the Son of God," Milton warned me at our first meeting. "Could I then just tell you why I believe He is?" I said. "OK," he said, reluctantly. Pointing out this precious truth from the Bible, I commenced teaching Milton the gospel of grace, and gave him lessons which he could teach his class. One night, I went to his house and found Milton weeping, his head bowed down on the dining room table. "I'm an unworthy sinner and don't deserve to be saved!" he cried. God graciously saved him that night.

Another blessing was the conversion of Air Force Sergeant Dale Green and his wife, June. Years before, as June's mother was dying, she made June put her hand under her hip (like Abraham had done with his servant in Genesis 24) and asked her to vow never to leave the Baptist church. Dale and June were heavy drinkers. One day some Mormons visited her at home and confused her. A neighbour told June to send for me. I met the Greens and they both agreed to come to the Sunday evening gospel meeting. "Please come visit us," Dale said after the meeting. "I'll be up tomorrow night." I replied.

Monday night I went to their house and opened the Scriptures to John 1:10-13. Verse 13 says, "But as many as received Him, to them gave He the power to become the sons of God, even to them that believe on His name." The Lord used these words as I tried to explain to Dale and June how to be saved by believing and receiving. All of a sudden Dale said, "June, I just got saved!" As he turned to his wife, his eyes flooded with tears. June began crying, too, and said, "And I was saved last night, and was afraid to tell you!" They hugged each other and cried. The liquor was poured down the kitchen drain.

However remembering her vow, June called for the military chaplain, himself a Baptist. He advised her, "If you got saved there you should stay there." So Dale and June entered the fellowship at the Northern Lights Boulevard Gospel Hall. After the big earthquake of 1964 Dale's unit was deployed back to Tennessee. The Lord increased the number in fellowship to 85. The judgement seat of Christ will reveal what was of God.

Our family increased too. On March 30, 1963, our fourth child, Brent, was born in Palmer, Alaska, on the day of our 17th wedding anniversary, and we rejoiced at the coming of another boy.

The old 1948 station wagon which we purchased in 1954 had served us well. However it was nearing the end of its effectiveness. God again exercised John and Edith MacLelland to purchase another car through her brother Jim, and send it up to us. It was a lovely Packard. They had it driven to Seattle and I arranged for it to be driven up to Alaska.

Assembly at Northern Lights, 1960

CHAPTER 12

The Earthquake

The Great Earthquake of 1964 of course brought many changes. The news of it made headlines around the world, reaching Northern Ireland and South Africa where our families lived. Graphic pictures of the damage and casualties caused them much concern. Our home was badly shaken, so much that the foundation blocks were crushed and the house was damaged. All the utilities were shut off and rendered useless. The Gospel Hall was still usable, so we opened it to those who had lost their homes. Since the telephone lines had been knocked down, we could not reach loved ones overseas. We were surprised, then, when suddenly our telephone rang. It was Jim Graham, my brother-in-law, calling from Belfast. "Are you all right?" he asked through the crackle of static and delay of the line. "Yes, all are safe," I replied. No sooner had those eight words been exchanged than the telephone line went dead. It remained so for several more weeks. Jim never received a bill from his phone company for that call. More miracles? Jim brought much relief to our friends and relatives in Ulster, and to those at the Belfast Easter conference when he told them the good news of our safety. Much praise ascended to the Lord.

One man from Canada, brother Reilly, attending that conference, wrote a letter and addressed it to "Tommy Thompson, Missionary, Alaska." He requested if I got his letter, please send him my address. I got the letter and replied to brother Reilly. He often wrote afterward and often enclosed a gift.

My parents in South Africa were very concerned when they heard about the earthquake. My father came to 2 Kings 4:26 in his daily reading. That verse describes Elisha instructing his servant Gehazi to inquire of the Shunammite woman, "Is it well with thee?" The Shunammite woman answered, "It is well."

"It is well!" my father shouted to my mother. "Aggie, they are all well!" "How do you know?" my mother asked. "From God's Word," he said. They both bowed their heads and thanked the Lord having heard nothing from us, yet receiving assurance through God's Word. This type of faith was passed on to me (2 Timothy 1:5). I am thankful to the Lord for such godly parents.

Many villages along the Alaskan coast were devastated either by the earthquake or the tsunami which it caused. In the days and weeks that followed, homeless villagers were brought to Anchorage and housed in schools that were not damaged too much. I was asked to supervise their welfare, and many of their needs were supplied by Christian friends of mine. However, when the Red Cross, which came from outside Alaska, found out I was also witnessing the gospel, my services were abruptly no longer needed.

I could now give time to rebuilding our home. We dumped Sadie's broken dishes into a wheel-barrow with other debris and took it all to the dump. After our foundation was repaired and our home set back in place, we discovered that the earthquake had displaced much ground underneath the house. This encouraged the boys to make a basement. They began digging out under the house with a metal can and called me to see it. They had removed so much that we were all encouraged to dig and soon had a basement under half of the house. Brian made his bedroom down there, as well as a small study. It is just like God to leave more room after an earthquake than before, at no extra cost!

The God of miracles preserved us physically through the earthquake in spite of the dangerous experiences we all had. As the quake shook the city, a young native mother named Shirley threw herself on top of her children to save them from a collapsing ceiling. Light from God suddenly showed her that Christ had done the same thing for her, sheltering her from death. Shirley was saved still sheltering her children from danger. She attended gospel meetings and Sunday School both in Chitina and then in Anchorage. But it is God alone that gives the increase and grants salvation. Her husband was an atheist. Her faith inflamed his anger and he began abusing her. Horribly, in a fit of rage, he stabbed her through her heart. It was a sad funeral which I took. I preached the gospel to many people through her testimony.

*　*　*　*　*

In 1965, we got word that my dad back in South Africa, Thomas James "Jimmy" Thompson, had passed home to glory shortly after praying during a week night. I received the news in Ketchikan where I was sharing gospel meetings with my childhood friend and fellow laborer in Alaska, John Abernathy. Reading from John 11:6 I noticed "two days", so I continued for two more nights before flying back to Anchorage. There waiting for me was a cheque for $5,000 in a letter, more than enough for us all to fly to South Africa return. I immediately booked round-trip flights on Air France to Cape Town for all the family.

Two days afterwards the telegram office telephoned me and asked me if I wished them to read another message. "Yes," I said. "Wrong cheque sent. Yours coming for $59. Sorry for mistake."

I felt the blood drain from my face and my jaw slackened. Fortunately I had not yet used the cheque to pay for the Air France tickets, so returning the money was no problem. But the tickets were booked and payment would be due shortly.

When I broke the news to Sadie, she began to laugh. "Oh, Tommy," she said, catching her breath. "I wish you could see the look on your face!" She always saw the humour in things and knew how to lighten up when I saw the sad side.

Sadie went shopping and took the boys. I went to the Lord in prayer. "Lord, I know I need humbled," I prayed. "But this is humiliation. What will I do?" The verse that came to my mind was Exodus 4:2 where God said to Moses, "What is that in thy hand?" I told the Lord about my car, worth $600, Brian's piano, worth $200, the fish bowl, $50, etc. I arose fully assured the Lord would open up the way. We needed $3,000 for the tickets, but we did not have that kind of money on hand. Sure enough, no sooner had I said "Amen" when the telephone rang. "Tommy, could you get us a car for our daughter?" It was Harold Richards. Just like that, the car was sold.

A few days later, an old friend, Julius Wuerth, heard from someone that I was going to South Africa. Years earlier, I had helped Julius avoid bankruptcy. He now owned a successful automobile dealership in Anchorage. He handed me $800. "You helped me, now I am helping you!" he said. The saints in the assembly gave us a gift of $400. Soon I had all except $600.

Air France called and said it was time to pay for the tickets. The day before the tickets were to be picked up, Harold Richards called to tell me they had sold a piece of property and had decided to give me the tithe. "It's only $600," he said. God again provided.

The tickets in our hands now, the mailman told me if we went to the post office early on the day of our departure, before he made his rounds, he would give us the mail due that day. Brian went down to the post office and brought back the mail. One letter caught our attention and we opened it. "Here is the $59 cheque," the letter read. "Sorry about the mistake." The Lord also gave us our pocket money for the trip. Hallelujah!

When we arrived in Cape Town and went to my mother's home, a sad sight met my eyes when I entered her bedroom. My dad's empty bed, Mother ill from shock with clots in her leg. I took it upon myself to wind up her affairs when she said, "Tommy take me back to Belfast." Again the Lord provided her fare through a legacy left me by a Miss Walker which just covered the cost.

We all arrived safely in Belfast and kindly were allowed the use of one of the missionary homes there while I tried to find accommodation somewhere for mother. I located a wee house in Cregagh Road area, and Jim my brother in law loaned me the difference to settle the deal.

When the Lord indicated for us to return to Alaska, we had one more family member than when we had left. On June 2, 1966, Sadie gave birth to our fifth child, an only daughter, Sarah Elizabeth, in Lisburn, Northern Ireland. We called her Bettie in honor of Sadie's sister. Our children were now Brian, Billy, Barry, Brent and Bettie: the five Bs.

Before leaving Belfast we settled my mother into the wee house in Cregagh Road. Albert Aiken helped me put electricity throughout the house. I also turned a little kitchen storage area into a bathroom, so we left her comfortable.

CHAPTER 13

New Developments

Back in Anchorage, the growing city was widening Northern Lights Boulevard and took 10 feet off our front parking lot. What was once just a dusty road at the edge of town had become an important east-west thoroughfare as the city expanded southward. When a car knocked down a girl crossing the road to attend our gospel meeting, we wondered what to do next.

Some months earlier, I had been offered land several miles south of the city in an undeveloped subdivision called Parkway Estates. I used some building maintenance savings to buy it for the Assembly. The seller also offered me a smaller plot adjacent to it, if we bought the lot. God had set the land before us, and we paid for it.

I drew up plans for a new building and began preparing the ground for the foundation. We sold the old hall to a printing company, so we had now $50,000 to build the new hall. I went to the cement block company to get cost estimates for materials to build the walls. "Is this for a church building?" the manager asked. When I said yes, he took me to see Mr. Frank who was administrating a federally-funded programme which was teaching Alaska natives to learn a trade of cement block laying. Mr Frank said, "Mr. Thompson, if you agree, our crew of students will do all the block-laying work for free. You see, I'm tired of using the same 100 blocks to teach the students. I'll supervise the block-building on your church."

Not surprisingly, Mr. Frank turned out to be a Christian from

Washington, D.C. on temporary duty. Under his tutelage and guidance, the native bricklaying students did a lovely job in a short time. I supervised and worked with some of the believers on all the other construction details. Vern Picket flew up from Arlington to do all the electrical work. Soon the assembly moved into Parkway Estates Gospel Hall, debt free.

My good friend, Carl Rylander, the contractor, helped me make some beautiful, upholstered pews out of lovely birch wood. We saw the Lord's hand of blessing in this place. The work prospered and souls were saved and even some restored.

I was having health problems and the Lord used this to send us back to South Africa shortly after moving into the new hall. We laboured in Cape Town and various other places for nearly two years. In 1972, I felt so much better due to the warm climate and decided to go back to Alaska.

On our return I was able to build a house on the plot next to the Gospel Hall which had been promised by the seller. Again it was another labour of love and soon we moved into a nice home with four bedrooms.

Less than 10 years after opening the doors of Parkway Estates Gospel Hall, the city of Anchorage grew to take in Parkway Estates and re-zoned it for light industrial use. The assembly was forced to make another move.

I went to see our old friend and former neighbor John Henry Graham who was a land developer. He had made a lot of money in real estate, so I went to inquire whether he had any land suitable for another Gospel Hall.

At that time, John Henry had no plots zoned for a church building. "But, you will need a plot of land personally, too, won't you?" he asked. When I said yes he offered me the plot next to his own house.

He and his wife, Norah, now lived in south Anchorage in a subdivision he had developed called Oceanview. Norah told her husband that she wanted the Thompsons to live next to them. John Henry actually handed me title to the plot of land next to his home, without payment.

We started building our house and had wonderful help from Vern and Helen Pickett, who along with their son Lawrence moved to Alaska from the state of Washington to help. Carl Rylander and several other friends helped, too.

Mr. Graham told us to take whatever lumber we needed from where he stored it next to his house. "When you finish, we will settle the cost," he said. So meticulously, I kept track of every piece of John Henry's lumber that was used. When we were finished with the house, I went over to his office with the book in which I had recorded the materials. When I asked him to tell me how much I needed to pay to settle the cost of materials, he just laughed. "Are you stupid?" he asked. I was mystified at that response. So I pressed him again and asked him to tell me, based on my careful records, how much I owed him. He just seemed unconcerned and non-committal. I did not know what to make of his attitude. He told me he was busy, took a telephone call and waved me out of his office. I left his office without an answer, feeling rather perturbed.

The answer came later when John Henry and Norah told me that some friends of mine had asked me to get them land in Oceanview. Through my referral, John Henry had sold it to them directly, without going through a real estate agent. It was an expensive piece of land and what John Henry pocketed on the transaction was significant. "Your lumber is already paid," John Henry declared.

Finally, John Henry called to tell me he had a piece of land on Dimond Boulevard which we could have for a church building. Once again, he handed me the title deeds without any money changing hands. We took the proceeds from the sale of the Parkway Estates Gospel Hall and applied it towards construction of Dimond Boulevard Gospel Hall. Many hands worked on the new building, and the assembly began meeting there in 1978. God's ways are beyond comprehension. I know now what Mr. Alfred Cuff meant when he wrote to me these words, "Faith is always tried, but never disappointed."

Norah attended gospel meetings in the new hall and was saved. Emphysema ended her life a short while after this. John Henry asked me to take her funeral. I faithfully witnessed to John, even up to two days before he died. He left no testimony of being saved, but God knows and we leave this to Him. John's will showed I was to take his funeral service in the Gospel Hall! I conducted his funeral in the Dimond Boulevard Gospel Hall and many prominent civic leaders attended, including the governor of Alaska, and mayor and senators of Anchorage. The gospel was clearly preached at John Henry's funeral.

Gospel Hall, Anchorage

CHAPTER 14

Indian Valley

While at a gospel conference in Vancouver, British Columbia, the mother and aunt of a young woman living in Alaska asked me to try to locate her. They said Sylvia was living about 25 miles south of Anchorage in a place called Bird Creek. I visited the area when I returned to Alaska, and located Sylvia at Bird Creek. At one time, Sylvia was in assembly fellowship. She had married a man who claimed to be a Christian and moved with him to Alaska. Alas, he turned out to be an abusive, domineering failure of a man. Returning from this visit from Bird Creek, I noticed an unused A-Frame building in nearby Indian Creek. It had a sign outside that identified it as the Valley Bible Chalet. Upon investigating its ownership, I discovered that the chalet belonged to a Gospel Mission, but was not used by them.

I arranged to rent the building from the Gospel Mission, and started a Gospel outreach witness to the residents of Indian Valley and Bird Creek. Within a couple years we were able to purchase the building. Sylvia attended faithfully until her husband moved them 140 miles away. The Lord saved some souls and a little assembly was started in the A-frame chalet. Bonnie Kelly was the first to profess. She had been a Mormon at one time, but her family soon moved her away from "this cult".

Mary was another one who was wonderfully saved. Raised a Roman Catholic, Mary and her boyfriend, John, came to me and asked me to marry them. They seemed to have turned away from their religion. I am careful about performing such a wedding. But, after talking to them carefully, everything seemed fine.

After the wedding, Mary attended the gospel meetings in the chalet and was saved. This resulted in John physically abusing her and finally he shot her because she was a Christian. This ended the marriage and he left Mary for another woman. At the time of writing, Mary is in faithful fellowship at the Anchorage assembly.

On another occasion I visited door-to-door in Girdwood, 40 miles south of Anchorage where the famed Alyeska Ski Resort is located. At one door, another lady named Bonnie accepted our invitation and began attending the gospel meetings in the chalet.

As we got to know her, she told us about the sad life she had lived. At a young age, Bonnie ran away from a sexually abusive step-father. She went to live in Miami, Florida. There she entered the world of drugs. But she always lamented and thought about her innocent life before her father died when she was 10 years old. She had come to Alaska to try to escape her cruel and dangerous drug life. However drugs were a weekend pleasure for many professional men at the Alyeska Ski Resort, and Bonnie soon got mixed up with the drug crowd again.

After our visit and invitation, Bonnie attended gospel meetings each week. After six weeks, she was wonderfully saved and baptised. Her thoughts turned to her young sister at home, so Bonnie left Alaska to rescue her from the step-father. A few years ago, I met Bonnie again 50 miles from Anchorage. She had married a good man, started a family and was attending a fundamental church. The reports I have heard about her since then are that she still goes on in her Christian life. She credits our ministry through the chalet for saving her and her life.

A man named Dallas ordered me off his property at gunpoint. I learned later that Dallas had shot a man who was stealing some fuel from his tank. He was reputed to shoot any dogs that strayed on to his property.

I left him alone, but continued visiting other cabins near him. Often when passing by, I would call out and ask him, "Are you doing any shooting today, Dallas?" He took the ribbing good-naturedly. Soon he would wave me to come and talk with him. He even removed the snow from the chalet parking lot with his snow removal truck, but he never attended any meetings.

A number of years later Dallas became seriously ill with cancer, so I went to visit him. "Tommy, will you pray for me?" he asked. He was so weak and thin from cancer that he needed constant attention. He could not lift his arms and his limbs, and needed daily massages to prevent further deterioration. My heart went out to him because death was near. I lifted my heart to heaven and the Lord gave me words suitable for Dallas. I was very disturbed that I had seen no results of this visit and went home deeply moved about his death so near and him not saved. Encouraged by Marjorie I returned the next day to visit him. When I entered he said to his son, "Come and hear what Tommy has to tell us."

I took him to Calvary. I described for him that it was there that the thief had cried out to Christ, "Lord! Remember me." I told Dallas that at that moment, Christ assured that criminal that his destiny was with Him in Heaven. My heart was so heavy, looking at Dallas possibly for the last time. Suddenly he lifted his weak, withered arms towards heaven. "Lord Jesus, save me!" Dallas cried as loud as his weak voice would let him.

Arms that were immobilized were now strong enough to

express his faith in the Lord Jesus Christ. I cried with joy all the way home. Shortly afterwards, Dallas went home to be with the Lord.

Another man named Naylor was the owner-operator of the combination bar, restaurant and motel at Bird Creek. His daughter and wife accepted an invitation to the gospel meetings at the Chalet and both professed salvation.

"Watch out for that blood-sucking preacher," Naylor warned them, referring to me. "He's only after money." I spoke with him about the things of the Lord, but he declared he had no need for it. After that he said to his family, "He's different than those blood suckers."

Fifteen years later, during Sadie's illness, Naylor was brought into the same hospital for an emergency heart operation. His family looked until they found me. When they found me, they were crying and asked me to come quickly to him. I accompanied him to the operating room, speaking to him all the way there about his soul.

God allowed Naylor to rally and get better. All this brought a change in his attitude. He loved me to visit him and read the Bible to him. He even gave me a massage support for my back when he heard I was having back trouble and much discomfort. When his condition took a turn for the worse and he was admitted to the hospital, it would be for the last time. I prayed with him and spoke tenderly of Christ's work on the cross.

"Tommy, how can I be saved?" he asked. "Believe on the Lord Jesus Christ, and thou shalt be saved,'" I said, quoting Acts 16:31, and simply told him what this meant. In that moment, on his deathbed, "twas done, the great transaction's done". Naylor was saved when he cried out "Lord save me."

At his funeral, I let a few of his friends speak about him. One old, hard sinner stood up and said, "Naylor is in heaven now; he told me he was saved when I visited him in hospital" - a real confirmation of Romans 10:9. This was a great comfort to me and all the family.

CHAPTER 15

Hospital Visitation

Hospital visitation has been a reaping place for me at times, too. In 1979, while Pope John Paul visited Anchorage, I was visiting patients in the Roman Catholic Sisters of Providence Hospital. Passing one room, I heard a man who was watching live coverage of the papal visit, let out a curse against the pope. I stopped and went into the man's room. He introduced himself as Lou.

"Are you an Ulster man?" I asked Lou. "Many of them do what you are doing." Lou said he was not from Ulster. Then he told a sad story about sexual abuse by a priest. That was the reason for his anger. He welcomed my visit, although he asked me, "Are you a priest?" I replied, "No, Lou, I am only a sinner saved by grace."

Lou said he was scheduled to have heart by-pass surgery. Bev Sullivan, a nurse in our assembly told me that the doctors could not find a good enough vein in his body. Late Sunday night, before his operation on Monday morning, I visited Lou. I had shared the gospel with him many times. Suddenly he said, "Tommy, I am scared of this operation. I might die." Getting down beside his bed I prayed aloud that God would show Lou that He loved him and would bring him safely through. At my "Amen" Lou said, "Tommy, I just got saved. I'm not afraid to die now."

He came through the operation. Two days later I was permitted to visit him. He was sitting up in a chair and doing very well, the nurse assured me. Lou became a greatly changed man - this was confirmed by people I knew from Kenai where he lived.

Beverly Sullivan is an experienced nurse in assembly fellowship. She has worked many years at Providence Hospital, and often alerts me to people that might benefit from my visits. Once I met two Christian ladies in the hospital's elevator. They were carrying a bouquet of brightly-colored balloons to give to their friend, Virginia, who had lost her foot because of diabetes. "But," the ladies told me, "She is so hard to witness to."

They gave me Virginia's room number. When I finished visiting the people I was there to see, I came to Virginia's room. "Do you know you can enter heaven without a foot?" I said loudly upon making my entrance.

"How do you know?" Virginia said immediately. I opened the Bible and read Matthew 18:8. "Wherefore, if thy hand or thy foot offends thee, cut them off and cast them from thee: it is better for thee to enter into life halt or maimed, rather than having two hands or two feet to be cast into everlasting fire." After several visits, Virginia professed Christ as Saviour.

Ceal was a cancer patient and a highly-educated woman. Her husband refused at first to permit me to visit her. One day I saw that he was not there. I knocked and entered Ceal's room. She wanted me to read the Scriptures. Soon she was to be discharged and asked me to visit her at home. Her husband also told me to feel free to visit anytime. During these visits, Ceal accepted Christ as her Savior.

We had sweet fellowship with her until she died. Her husband asked me to take the funeral and help him with all the affairs of it. In the course of the funeral arrangements, the funeral director suggested he could place things in the casket for her to take with her. "I have told my family to put my fishing rod in with me in case I go to hell!" the funeral director said. I strongly rebuked him. "Sir, there is no water in hell," I said, reminding him about the parable of the rich man in hell described in Luke 16:24. Many upper-crust educators and local leaders attended Ceal's funeral and heard how Ceal was assured of a home in heaven.

Later that year I traveled to speak at a conference in Vancouver, British Columbia. In my message, I referred to the "no water in hell" episode I had with the funeral director. One young lady who was just visiting at the conference with friends became so disturbed by that statement that she refused to drive home until she had peace with God, and she got saved. A little seed brought much fruit.

CHAPTER 16

Sad Farewells

In 1982, I received word that my mother, Agnes Crooks Thompson, was going blind. I had helped to return her to my sister Eileen in South Africa and I had a longing to go to see her. We put this before the Lord and the results were wonderfully worked out.

The man who had bought our house on speculation asked for a six-month extension on his agreement to pay $ 5,000 he owed, but he said he could not meet this commitment, and we were disappointed. When the crisis of my mother's health came up, I telephoned this man and asked him to accelerate his payment. He said, "No." Reluctantly, I then told him I would be forced to sell at a discount the parcels of real estate he had given to me for collateral. The next day he paid up in full.

Sadie, Bettie and I flew to South Africa and visited my mother. It was an enjoyable six weeks of happy fellowship with her and the beloved saints of the Cape Province. It was a sad parting from her and I'll remember it forever and her parting words: "Tommy go forth and preach the Gospel. You made your Daddy very pleased when he lived. Now do the same for the Lord and me!"

On the way back to Alaska, we stopped overnight in Amsterdam. The phone rang in our hotel room. My son, Billy, was on the line to let me know that my mother had gone to be with the Lord.

As soon as we could, we began to make arrangements for me to fly back to Cape Town for the funeral. Since it was a weekend, the airline would only give credit of $500. We decided it was best if Sadie and Bettie continued to Alaska.

I quickly ran into logistical problems with the airline. Although they assured me they would honor my passage to Alaska when I returned from South Africa, they would not issue a return to Cape Town. The KLM assistant agreed to let me use their telephone to call my brother George in Cape Town to see if he could do anything from that end. But, because it was the weekend, he could not help either.

Missionary pioneers can be stubborn, and I was determined I was going back to Cape Town on the 5 pm. South Africa Airline flight. I put my luggage in a cart and decided to go through the same way as the KLM assistant had taken me, right past the elevated immigration booth, without stopping.

Just as I neared the office door inside the immigration booth, an officer (angel?) called out, "Can I help you sir?" Then he pushed my luggage all the way through and past the booth and barriers without question. He pointed me to the place where I could meet the South Africa Airline pilot. My heart was beating very fast by now.

I saw a South Africa Airline official approaching my location. He was not the pilot, but was the station manager. I explained to him what I was trying to do. Quickly, he wrote down my credit card and, using his own credit card, covered my round-trip to Cape Town. "Run quickly!" he told me. "The flight is leaving in 10 minutes."

I charged through the airport to the gate as fast as I could. Thankfully, the door to the aircraft was still open and I squeezed in. I plopped down, exhausted, in a back seat. I had no sooner sat down when a lady told me she had just been assigned that seat. I moved over. The lady sat down and began to weep. I asked her what was the matter? "I have just spent four months with my sick mother, and now I have to return home," she said. "I am so afraid that I will never see her again."

I told her about my mother just passing away and the great effort I had made to return to Cape Town for her funeral. "But look at your face compared to mine," she said, and an inquisitive look of wonder passed over her face. I replied, "I am at peace because I know my mother is in heaven." This opened the great subject of assurance and the gospel. I pointed her to the Bible and let her read reassuring verses.

A 14-hour trip lay before us. At that time, most African nations banned South Africa Airlines from flying through their air space, so our flight path was particularly circuitous.

After take-off, I tried to get some sleep, but I was constantly awakened by the lady next to me as she sought answers to many questions. One part of me secretly hoped she would fall asleep, too. But she wanted Bible answers to her questions. Commiting my situation into the Lord's hands, I showed her the answers from Scriptures. When the aircraft stopped for refueling she asked me to go outside with her, which I reluctantly agreed to do. After take off I answered several questions. Because of the hectic day I went fast asleep.

Two hours from Johannesburg, the flight crew awakened us for breakfast. I was groggy by this time. The last thing I wanted was the lady next to me to tap my arm again. But she did, and this time something seemed different about her. "Mr. Thompson," she said excitedly. "I just got saved, and now I know I will go to heaven when I die. I also will write to my mother and share this with her."

God moves in mysterious ways indeed. I thought I had somehow missed the mind of God in all the fuss in Amsterdam.

Now I knew God planned it all for His glory, surely His ways are past finding out!

My return to Cape Town, although very sad in one way, was joyous because I knew mother was now with my father at home with the Lord. That's what she longed for after he died. Mother always wanted her whole family to be near her, and we were all together at her funeral. In retrospect, it was the last time all four of us were together at the same place on this side of heaven. Andy, Eileen and George have all since passed on.

On my return journey I had a stopover at the Johannesburg airport, so I telephoned the lady I had met on the flight from Amsterdam. "Mr. Thompson, you will be glad to know I was at the Baptist Easter service this morning celebrating my Lord's resurrection!" she said with genuine delight in her voice.

God often opens the door, but we have to walk through with fear and trembling, even if we have to push through with our luggage in a carrier, breaking the law. But the Bible does say, "Fear God and honour the King".

* * * * *

In January 1984, Sadie and I flew to Seattle for a Bible conference. We took the opportunity to get medical check-ups at the Medical Center owned by Stewards' Foundation. I got a cleared report by the hospital. Things were different, however, for Sadie. X-rays showed some shadowing on one of her lungs.

The doctors administered tuberculosis medications to treat her for every possible cause of the shadowing. These made her very sick and weak. I took her to Westport on the coast to await the results of several other tests the doctors ordered.

After Sadie fell asleep in the hotel bedroom on the coast, I went for a walk along the wharf and prayed earnestly, beseeching the Lord to make her better. But it was Ezekiel 24:16 that came to my mind. In that passage, the Lord told Ezekiel of the imminent death of the prophet's wife. God warned Ezekiel, "Son of man, behold, I am about to take from thee the desire of thine eyes." I ran along the wharf with my hands covering my ears, shouting over the crash of the waves. "No Lord!" I shouted. "No!"

Later, back in Seattle, we were eating breakfast in the home of our hosts, dear friends Dave and Sandy Brandt. It was January 28, 1984. The telephone rang. It was Sadie's doctor. I took the call. "Please sit down. I have some news to tell you," the doctor said. "I'm sorry, but Sadie has incurable cancer in her right lung."

My mind reeled with shock. How will I tell Sadie? There was no use in delaying, so I simply told her what the doctor had said. "Well, Tommy," she said softly like the faithful soldier she ever was. "We will wait and see."

It's impossible to describe the dark clouds that filled our hearts. Dave and Sandy were so kind and comforting. The flight back to Anchorage was one of mixed emotions because the family had to be told of this awful news about their mother.

The whole family was stunned, but rallied around us. Brian was super-good to us. Billy flew back from his job on the South Sea island of Pago Pago where he was supervising the construction of airfields and docks. Billy put $6,000 at our disposal. Barry, who lived in Johannesburg, took it hard. Brent flew back from visiting Barry in South Africa. Young Bettie, not yet 18 years old and set to graduate from high school in May, was shocked.

The next six months were a blur of therapy, radiation treatments, hospital visits, and doctors' appointments. An operation was attempted, but the surgeon had no sooner looked inside Sadie when he simply called off the procedure. The cancer had metastasized. Now all hopes were dashed and it was just a matter of time. In the final stages, Sadie was provided with nursing care in our own home. A few days before she died, I was sitting with her. With what little breath she had, she turned to me. "Tommy," she said. "I'm up here, looking down on that body. I'm not in it." I thought of the glory of God described in Ezekiel 10:4 and 11:22, 23, slowly ascending and leaving Jerusalem.

Barry flew in from South Africa upon receiving our reports that Sadie did not have long to live. He went into her room and visited his Mum. When he left, she asked, "Is Barry gone?"

Having seen all her children, Sadie seemed from that point to surrender herself to the Lord to take her Home. She was a wonderful soldier in submission to the Lord's will. On the July 31, 1984, at 1 pm., Sadie departed for her Home above. She was 56 years old. We had been married for 39 years.

Brian sums it up perfectly when he says, "Mum showed us how to live and also how to die." Oh, how we all missed Sadie: a great wife, mother of five, and fellow-soldier.

I will not write of everything about those awful months after Sadie's passing. A few things stand out, though. When I read Ephesians 5:20 about "giving thanks always for all things", I must confess my inability to do this regarding my dear Sadie. I wrestled with my inability to give thanks for Sadie's illness. I had never before felt such lack of understanding of God's will and His Word. One day during this struggle, I read 1 Thessalonians 5:18: "In everything give thanks, for this is the will of God in Christ Jesus concerning you." Of course, I had read that verse many times before, but like a bolt, that first word, *in* glowed into my mind, as I read it again, emphasizing that first word. With tears of thankfulness to the Lord, I finally understood. It was not for me so much to give thanks *for* Sadie's illness as much as it was for me to give thanks *in* the trial.

Reviewing the whole past experience of Sadie's cancer, I could give thanks for things *in* the trial, for many experiences including the kindness of Dave & Sandy Brandt in Seattle. Then Sadie's primary physician, Dr. Beth Baker, had given us her home telephone number. "Call me anytime and I will come." Doctors don't generally make home visits anymore. Yet we could be thankful that Dr. Baker was willing and available to come anytime. The pharmacist had said, "Call me at any hour and I'll come down to the pharmacy and give you what Sadie needs" - another most unusual kindness.

Brian took both Sadie and myself into his home every Friday night, fed us dinner (he is a talented cook), and put us to bed in his guest bedroom. This he did until Sadie was not able to go out. I hate to remember, though, I often had to slip out and go back home for clean clothes because of the sweat of stress. But the comfort, kindness and care Brian gave made our trial easier to bear, and Sadie got so much comfort out of Brian's attention.

Near the end, night nurses were provided for Sadie's care, and that was a welcome relief. One senior nurse was a particular comfort because of her expertise, so that even Dr. Baker listened to her advice and suggestions.

This nurse was an agnostic. I spoke to her about the reality of God, salvation through Christ, and other such things. "Why don't you ask God to show you that He is real?" I challenged her.

One day, she and her disabled husband drove their pickup truck to a river to fish. When they were finished fishing, she noticed the fuel gauge in the truck was on empty. The highway was 16 miles away, so walking out was not an option. Besides, she couldn't leave her disabled husband there alone because of the danger from bears. Remembering my challenge to her about God, she bowed her head and asked God to please take them to the main road for help. She started the engine, and began driving back.

God did better than she asked. With the fuel gauge never moving off "empty", God took them to a filling station 20 miles away. Just as she turned the truck into the station, the engine stuttered and stalled to a halt, out of fuel.

She related this whole episode to me on her next visit to our house. God had manifested His reality to her. I then counseled and even warned her of her personal need to believe on the Lord Jesus for salvation. As far as I know she did not make a profession of faith. After Sadie died I never saw this nurse again. Many people wrote to me about how the Lord used Sadie's death to bring glory to Himself.

Mothers are often the glue of the family, and Sadie's departure proved this to be true. The finality of her absence brought on an awful loneliness. I struggled to deal with the reality of never seeing her again on earth. I threw myself into working long hours putting in new foundations at the Indian Valley Chalet. I would eat breakfast, take an apple, a sandwich and some water for my lunch, and work late into the evening. This physical labor was a therapy indeed.

I had Bettie, my dear daughter, to console. It hurt me so very much to see her missing her mother. Every day during Sadie's illness, Bettie would sit with her and talk about many things. I often heard them laugh. A daughter's loss of her mother, especially at such a young age, brings unique pain.

I decided to visited Ulster for Christmas and brought Bettie and Brian with me. I found myself going to familiar spots Sadie and I cherished in our younger days. This was so hurtful, and perhaps not wise. "What are you here for?" I asked myself at one of these spots. "I'm looking for Sadie," I replied to myself. This realization brought sobs of pain.

The Lord comforted me in many ways. On the way to Wallace Avenue Assembly in Lisburn for the Lord's Day's meetings they had asked me to take, I pulled my car down a side street and cried, "Lord, if I you could show Sadie to me in heaven, then I could go through with the meetings at the assembly." I prayed this but please don't think this request is foolish if you have not passed through such a trial.

The meeting began, and the first brother to pray took us into God's very presence. Somehow his prayer was deep with expressions of the presence and mystery of God. This surely was an answer to my cry! It turned out that the brother who prayed had been through a great family trial himself, and this was the first time in six months he had taken part in public prayer.

When I got up to preach, I experienced a nearness of the Lord that I had not felt in a long, long time. When four elders approached me after the Gospel meeting, this brother was the one who spoke. "Brother Tommy," he said, "I enjoyed your message. If I had not been saved already, I would have been saved tonight." At that moment, I hesitated to tell him how his prayer had strengthened me. But a little later I went to the cloak room. He was there getting his coat, too. "Brother," I said, "You should know that your prayer was of great help and encouragement to me today," and I related my early morning experience. We just wept on each other's shoulders and never said another word. But God brought comfort to both of us that day.

* * * * *

In 1986, after two years alone, the Lord brought into my life my dear Marjorie to be my wife. She has proved a helpmeet in the fullest sense of that word. She labours beside me, and on her own especially in the needs associated with the Lord's assembly in Anchorage.

I thank the Lord that through Marjorie I have again enjoyed

being devoted to the work the Lord has placed in our hands. After the loss of Sadie, my service to the Lord sometimes felt more like a duty rather than devotion, if one can understand the difference.

Marjorie is very much her own, ladylike person. The place she has taken has not been easy for her. She left a good career and a happy family, plus a number of assemblies in her home area in New Jersey and Pennsylvania, to move to Alaska. She has indeed sacrificed much to come into the Thompson family. Marjorie has made me live again, as it were, and shares the burden of the work of the Lord with me.

I can say the assembly in Anchorage has good potential in mostly young families and young believers. While I have planted and watered, God has given the increase in spite of plenty of opposition over the years.

In December 2004 eleven believers who had been in fellowship in the Anchorage assembly and lived in Wasilla, planted an assembly in His Name in Wasilla. It is 55 miles from Anchorage and is the fastest growing area in Alaska. Two of the main men are my spiritual sons in Christ. I always felt there should have been a testimony to His Name there many years ago and now the Lord has answered our prayers.

I have served my own generation by the will of God. Like Caleb (I am fast approaching his age recorded in Joshua 14:10-11) I can say, "If the Lord will be with me, then I shall be able" to go wherever He may yet lead us in the time allocated by His grace.

APPENDIX 1

How God Saved Me

by Pat Bell, Alaska

I was born on 14th August, 1914 in Chitina, Alaska and grew up in the customs and ways of my people, the Athabascan Indians of North America. My mother died when I was still a young boy. I ran away from home when I was eight. For my sinful young life I was always being sent away from Chitina and eventually, when I was thirteen, they sent me to Idaho to St. Anthony Industrial Training School.

I behaved myself good and they gave me a Bible for that, but I spoiled this when I was found out smoking my first cigarette.

May month 1934 Spring, I got off the train at Chitina. It was the Copper River and North Western Railway. (When I got off at my old home town I never thought I would have a feeling for touching alcohol. By that time I had disliked it.) All my friends in town were waiting for the train. Soon as I stepped out everyone came to shake my hand. I had two fine adopted sisters who came and walked home with me. I was very glad to see them. And there was my old Dad, working unloading the mail and freight. He had been on the railroad for twenty years. Even when it was shut down because of no more work at Kennecott Mine, he worked til they closed the railroad.

The same train I came in brought a carload of whisky, beer and wine. The liquor store had been set up in town - that was something new. On my first trip to town I met my old gang who had grown up with me in this little home town of Chitina. (The word Chitina come from native language. Chitty is Copper Rocks and na means river or streams. "Chitty na" that's how it got its name Chitina, pronounced Chit-na.)

But now to get back to my going to town. That's when I met my old gang and to my surprise they each had a bottle of liquor and all of them offered me to join them. But I refused to take anything for I did not like the taste. (For years the drinking had been going on and whenever I came home there were drinking parties going on.) One night two years after, in 1936, I felt lonely and blue, longing for what we thought was a good time. Two of my friends were living close to my home in our native village so I go and visit them. I come up to the door and knocked, no one answered. I had in mind that I am going to join them and take a little drink. The one who owned the house opened the door slowly and let me in. There was a young lady there who was very drunk and she set up a glass for me. It was pretty strong. This first drink I ever took and it got me into trouble for fighting so I had to serve ten days for being drunk and disorderly. In jail I thought I would never touch liquor again. But when I was released from jail I met some of the old gang and I was glad to see them again. We all went to town and onto a spree. This was my life for a long time after.

I didn't like the life I was leading. The liquor had gotten me into all kinds of big troubles. Once it was very serious trouble when I had frozen my feet. I had gotten six months for robbing a whisky cache, which I drank, and found guilty was sent away to jail. On my way back I had left Anchorage on the mail truck bound for Chitina. Another guy was with me who owed me money and for that he bought me a gallon of wine. I took a little too much. When the mail truck stopped at Lower Tonsina, fifteen miles from Chitina so they could put chains on the wheels as the hill was very icy and slippery, I got into argument with a new passenger, so I walked away from the truck. I was so drunk that I did not know where I was going and got lost in the bush. Walking on an ice covered stream, I thought it was strong, but when I stepped on the ice I broke through and found myself with no shoe on one foot. Not remembering where I left it, I kept on going, wet up to the waist, very cold and tired. I went through some brush and soon I came up to the road. I looked down about fifty feet and there was a house. I was so glad I ran and knocked for five minutes. My foot was freezing pretty bad. Just then the door opened and a nice, kind, young cripped lady opened the door and let me in. It was 5.30 in the morning. She soon made a fire to warm me up but when she felt my foot she said, "It is frozen hard as a rock." I was so worried for there was nothing we could do at all for my foot. This lady was Hattie Mack. She had a jar of Vicks so she put that on and I was taken back to Anchorage again. The old doctor at Providence Hospital said, "It's a good thing you put Vicks on. It helped."

I was in hospital for nearly two months and my foot healed. I was now a heavy drinker and worked only to drink. Now out of hospital I spent the day getting drunk.

The Second World War years I spent in Cordova and now I was a real alcoholic and not able to quit. After the war I got back to Chitina. Most of the boys and girls I knew before had gotten married and Chitina itself had changed. The family had changed too. By Summer 1954 I got worse and now felt sick too - but Satan gave me more and more.

When the new missionary came, he asked me to meetings and he preached good and I heard good - for now I was deaf too. I was member of Russian Orthodox Church all my life, and it also was my old Dad's church.

The chart used by Mr. Thompson taught me that Christ alone can free me from Satan's power. Now I want to be saved real bad, but still I drink and get blue and very sad - but I keep putting it off.

On December 21, 1954 I got up after the meeting and went to the missionary and told him, "I want to be saved." He read a verse from the Bible, one in 1 Timothy 1:15 "this is a faithful saying ... Christ Jesus came into the world to save sinners." He made me understand very well. He had given me a paper to read some time before this, "Old John is Dead, I'm new John." Now I want to be new Pat, so I bowed down and asked Jesus to save me. That night I walked out of the hall at Chitina feeling really happy like a new man. It was so different and I was so happy. I went around and told my friends, "Old Pat is dead. I'm new Pat."

Now I thank God, what a wonderful life this is, for I am with other Christians and have been baptised and breaking bread, remembering the way Jesus died. I am so happy.

When I look at those who are still drinking, I bend down on my knees and pray for them, also my old Dad. He was a real heavy drinker but now praying real with all his power too, having accepted the Lord into his heart just a little time ago.

The end

Pat Bell

Footnote
I had the joy of seeing Pat saved, and shepherded this dear soul until his earthly journey ended through sickness, placing his body in earth at Copper Center, Alaska, there to await the coming of the Lord.

Dear sinner, does this not encourage you to turn to the Saviour who did so much for Pat?

> Oh come, sinner, come to mercy's call
> Here at Jesus'feet;
> Oh come and repenting lay thine all
> Here at Jesus 'feet.
> Oh lay it down, lay it down,
> Lay thy weary burden down,
>> Oh lay it down, lay it down,
>> Down at Jesus'feet.

> Your servant for Jesus' sake,
>
> T.J. Thompson

Oh Serve the Lord with Gladness

Not in an earthly palace,
But in a humble stall,
Ye view the Lord of Heaven,
Wrapped in a swaddling shawl.

Not in an earthly palace,
But in the unnamed place,
Ye view the Lord of glory,
And marvel at His grace.

Not in an earthly palace,
But in the cottage home,
Ye view the Lord of comfort
Calm Martha's grief and groan.

Not in an earthly palace,
But on the tree of shame,
Ye view the Lord of mercy
Who settled all God's claims.

Oh give to Him thy homage,
And give to Him thy praise,
Who by His death of suffering
From sin, we He hath raised.

Lord such is our weak effort,
Like vapour so our days.
Grant grace and power to serve Thee,
And live unto Thy praise.

T.J. Thompson